Journey up the River

A Wayside Shrine—Mt. Adams

Anne Husted Burleigh

Journey up the River

A Midwesterner's Spiritual Pilgrimage

For John and Sheila,

In gratitude for your
faithfulness and
inspiration to families,

With best wishes,

Anne Husted Burleigh

IGNATIUS PRESS   SAN FRANCISCO

Cover art by Edward T. Hurley

Cover design by Riz Boncan Marsella

© 1994 Ignatius Press, San Francisco
ISBN 0–89870–468–5
Library of Congress catalogue number 94–77461
Printed in the United States of America

For my husband and children,
my parents, and
my brother and his family.

Contents

The Pilgrim's Prologue

Each one of us is the Lord's pilgrim. Plodding our path toward home, each of us is in transit across the world, invited to carry on the Lord's mission and then, finally, to move on to the heavenly city. From birth to death we are traveling through the Lord's history. Both the same being and yet never the same from one moment to the next, we are ever older than before, ever better or worse in health, in wealth, and in the order of our souls.

Our journey is universal; no one escapes it. To be human is to be on the way—to appear first in the world as a baby, then to grow through childhood, adolescence, adulthood, in successively more profound recognitions of the divine source of our life, and to go out, we hope, having lived responsibly our mission to reverence God and the world that he created. Time is our medium for this enterprise, for we see the fullness of being not all at once but only as we discover it over time. Time is the Lord's gift to us pilgrims, time in which we may praise, reverence, and serve God our Lord before we become finally happy with him in heaven.

Within our universal vocation to be pilgrims on the way to the heavenly city there are countless specific vocations. One of these vocations, because we are a historical people in time, is that of observer and record keeper of the race. Observers serve as the night watch. They live quietly, these watchful ones, marking their time in no way more extraordinary than to note the ordinary.

These observers and record keepers are temperamentally a bit detached. Though they live in the ordinary ways of everyone else, they keep one foot outside their own lives so that they can make notes in the margins. Whatever happens to them and to those around them they want to record, to stop in motion, to observe before it transmutes into another form.

As they watch over the coming in of life and the going out and much of the in between, they may, if they believe, look and listen for the Lord's voice in the great drama. Yet, because revelation is such a dramatic surprise, they do not know in what form the voice will come. And so they watch and wait for the hushed hovering wings of the Holy Spirit, looking for signs, fearful that if they go to sleep, they will miss the unfolding, perhaps missing the unfolding of which they themselves are some small part. They know that if they miss a second of the unfolding, they forever have missed that moment. The world does not circle back upon itself. On and on it goes forward, created, loved, scarred, and weary but redeemed, a strange, mysterious array of unfathomable providence, freedom, and contingency. Sin and sorrow and suffering weight it down, but every morning a silver light creeps up over the eastern horizon. Every morning is a morning of the Eighth Day.

In hope, in terror, in heartbroken joy the observers, the people of the night watch, wait for the shaft of light in the east. They keep records, aspiring to nothing so grand as a poetic vision of creation but merely hoping that if their records could be laid out end to end, some visionary could see in them the tracing of God's finger. Not a poet or mystic or philosopher is one of these watchful people but a scribe, whose modest calling requires him not to create but to stand by and take notes. The evangelist Matthew at the close of his Gospel defined this scribe, and the passage is admittedly mysterious. After telling to his disciples several parables about the kingdom of heaven, Jesus asked them, " 'Have you understood all this?' They said, 'Yes.' And he said to them, 'Well, then, every scribe who becomes a disciple of the kingdom is like a householder who brings out from his storeroom things both old and new.' "

Strange, this remark about a scribe to disciples who for the most part were barely, if at all, literate. Yet Jesus seems somehow to associate these disciples with the scribe, which indicates that the scribe is to write down or pass on the truth that he hears. If he does write the truth—which is the essence of his task—then he becomes a disciple of God's kingdom. And if he is a disciple of the kingdom, he is also a householder, that is, a member of the community of believers. As a householder he watches over his storeroom, which contains the treasury of the tradition he has received. In that storeroom are the old things of the Jewish patrimony and the new things that are the Gospel revelation.

The scribe, then, in guarding and conserving God's household, is to write the truth—not a truth that he makes up or judges for himself but the truth of God's revelation of himself in the world. The scribe is not to invent but only to record, to report, and in order to do so he must stand aside from the scene just enough to gain perspective on what is going on. Moreover, as Jesus implies, *only* if the scribe becomes a disciple of the kingdom does he have the chance to glimpse the truth in its fullness. Faith leads the way to understanding. Thus knowledge without faith is not full knowledge but is simply a shadow or an imitation of understanding. Unless the scribe is a disciple he will have no chance to see the fullness of God's hand in the creation. Unless he is a disciple he will not assume the householder's trusteeship of the creation, the creation that, like the householder, he guards as a vast storeroom of God's bounty.

As a disciple of the kingdom, the scribe is to have the prudence and sobriety of the householder, who keeps regular order of the provisions in his store-room, who conserves and guards the gifts of the household of God's kingdom. Like the householder, the scribe conserves both the valuable old things of the family tradition and also lays by the stores to accommodate the family in the future. Like the prudent householder, the scribe strives to use wisely both the old and the new, calling upon the greatest traditions in his history and also looking with hope to the future.

Might I be a scribe of the kingdom? It is possible; I will never know, however, until I reach the hindsight of heaven and can look back upon my life to see it as a whole. What is clear now is simply that for one for whom the poet or the mystic or the philosopher is beyond grasp, a certainty I have learned from hard experience, the far more modest scribe who has become a disciple is a good model. And, for one who by temperament and background considers our incarnation in history as the natural way to see ourselves, the record-keeping scribe is the logical model. If life is a pilgrimage, not a stationary, predetermined structure, then it is natural for a scribe to be taking notes on the journey, recording some facts on which we may later look back and reflect.

I have come to see my life as the slow, plodding

journey of a pilgrim, and for that I am grateful. If along the way I may sometimes act as a scribe, I am grateful for that, too. For it is not simply my own doings, I hope, that I record but also the meeting of Christ with a pilgrim on the way home. What I offer in this book, then, is not an autobiography. It is meant rather as a series of jottings on the spiritual journey common to us all but here particularized in the life of one woman. At times these reflections are more personal, at times more abstract. That juxtaposition of concrete and abstract mirrors life itself, in which we are at times immersed in experience or at other times fine-tuning the ideas that grow out of our experiences. The ideas—mine, certainly—are never perfected, for we continually receive new light that amplifies the meaning of our journey. Our ideas, like life itself, meander a great deal before they reach their goal. In this continuing meandering spiritual journey the constant symbol for me has been the river.

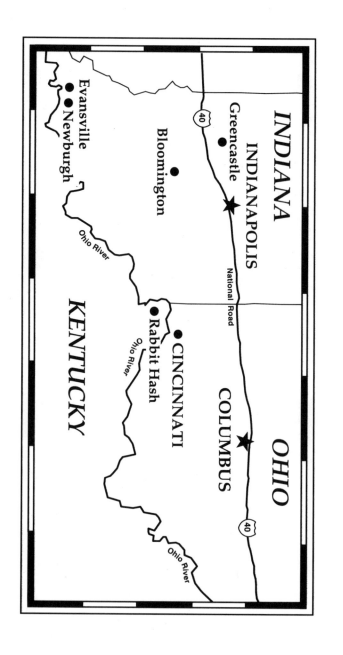

Chapter I

The River

A hundred and seventy-five years ago there swept over this country a Great Migration. Settlers from the East streamed forth in those years from 1815 to 1840, pouring into the new states carved from that remarkable creation of the Confederation Congress called the Northwest Territory.

At the beginning of that twenty-five-year migration America was still clustered east of the Appalachians, with only a few pockets of civilization in Kentucky and Tennessee and in the Old Northwest. At the beginning of those years there was but one state in the Old Northwest—Ohio. Indiana would enter the Union almost immediately, followed shortly by Illinois. But at the end of the period the Old Northwest was fast becoming the Midwest— heartland, robust, steady, the nurturing place for a distinctively American character.

The pioneers could choose one of two main routes into the Northwest, either the National Road or the

Ohio River. My ancestors, all of whom moved westward in the Great Migration, came by both avenues from their various homes in Vermont, New Jersey, or Virginia. Those settlers who journeyed along the northern route took the National Road, also known as the Cumberland Road. This first federal highway, U.S. 40, began at Cumberland, Maryland, where it followed the old military path of Braddock's Road as far as Laurel Hill in the Alleghenies, and then stretched on to Brownsville, Pennsylvania, on the Monongahela; to Washington, Pennsylvania; and to Wheeling on the Ohio River. By 1817 a semblance of a road was open to Wheeling. Eventually it would thrust as far west as Vandalia, Illinois, cutting through Cambridge and Columbus, then Richmond, Indianapolis, and Terre Haute. To call it a highway would be a euphemism. At best it was an unpaved country road; at worst it was hardly more than a track from which timber had been cut but had not been cleared of stumps. Wagon wheels cut ruts so deep that axles could snap or a horse carrying the mail could break a leg. The push for roads into the wilderness was so great, however, and the need so urgent to haul people, freight, and mail to the western settlements that the National Road became in its day an exemplary highway. Its eastern sections were macadamized—that is, paved with crushed stone and waterproof mortar. Especially in summer and early fall, when the rivers were dangerously low, the roads into the West—the National Road most of all—were indispensable.

But the greatest of all paths to the Old Northwest was the Ohio River. "La Belle Rivière" of the French, it formed not only the lower boundary of the lands of the Northwest Territory but also the southern highway into the wilderness. From its source at the confluence of the Allegheny and Monongahela Rivers at Pittsburgh it dropped a thousand miles to Cairo. It drained other rivers—the Muskingum at Marietta, the Scioto at Portsmouth, the Little Miami and Great Miami at Cincinnati, the Wabash below Evansville.

Every year during the spring rains the settlers gathered at Pittsburgh. Rumbling and clattering overland by way of Forbes' Road from Philadelphia, Braddock's Road from Cumberland on the Potomac, or the Genesee Road from Albany past the Finger Lakes, they collected in the bustling young city, jamming the town's boatmakers with orders for all kinds of river conveyances. Every sort of contraption went down the Ohio—flatboat, barge, ark, keelboat— whatever the owner could afford to accommodate his brood of wife, children, a yapping dog or two, chickens, hogs, cattle, household goods, tools, plow. From Pittsburgh the settlers ventured down the muddy, roiling Ohio, headed for Ohio, Indiana, or Illinois. If they were migrating from Virginia or the Middle

States, however, they often came by way of the southern path to the Northwest—down the Great Valley of Virginia, thence up through the Cumberland Gap, and along Kentucky's Wilderness Road to the Falls at Louisville, where they met the Ohio and continued downriver.

The two primary highways to the Old Northwest—the National Road and the Ohio River—carried both my paternal and maternal ancestors. Although some of the family paused in Ohio, most settled permanently in Indiana. None settled farther west than just over the Illinois line. Most of my paternal ancestors are buried in the little Auburn Methodist churchyard on Highway 40, the National Road, just west of Terre Haute. Many of my maternal ancestors are buried in Crown Hill in Indianapolis, only a few miles north of the National Road.

The paths that brought my ancestors to the Midwest and contained them there are likewise the very limits of my own life. By temperament and by circumstance I have never moved beyond the original boundaries marked off by my pioneer ancestors. By temperament and by circumstance I am so much a Midwesterner that I doubt my capacity to thrive outside the Midwest and, even more specifically, my own circumscribed region of the Midwest—the central and southern belt of Indiana extending south to the Ohio Valley and running from the southwestern toe of Indiana along the Ohio River as far northeast as Cincinnati. Bounded by the National Road on the north and the Ohio River on the south, I have lived my entire life within the confines laid out by the ancestors who came before me. I grew up within a few blocks of the National Road, known in Indianapolis as Washington Street. Even my schooling took place close by. Mrs. Baker operated my kindergarten in an old house one block north of Washington; Anna Pearl Hamilton Public School 77 was three blocks north; Thomas Carr Howe High School stood on a hill just above that street. When I went to college, I traveled only an hour west of Indianapolis to DePauw, just five miles north of the National Road. My graduate school, Indiana University at Bloomington, was no more than fifty miles south of it. And through the years when I was growing up, the meeting place in downtown Indianapolis was under the Ayres' clock at the corner of Meridian and Washington, where the north-south artery meets U.S. 40, the National Road.

When I married, my focus shifted to the southern boundary of my ancestors, the Ohio River. I have spent all my married life as close as a few yards from the riverbank and always within a whistle call of the *Delta Queen*. In nearly three decades I have lived in two river communities: Newburgh, Indiana, and Cincinnati, Ohio.

As the geography of my life has unfolded, the points on my map form a triangle: Indianapolis in the center of Indiana; Newburgh on the Ohio, almost in the toe of Indiana, where it borders on both Kentucky and Illinois; and Cincinnati, upriver just over the Ohio state line. My life very nearly has been lived within the limits of the triangle and very nearly—but not quite—within the boundaries of Indiana.

And so it is a contained life, a life drawn by lines, limited, defined, a life rooted in, dependent on place. It is a private life, a domestic life in which there has been considerable movement of the spirit but little physical movement from place to place. Yet it is in the private world, away from the public gaze and the eye of the state, where significant things happen to people—where they learn about the whole world; where they read and study; where they fall in love, marry, conceive babies, rear their children; where they gather with family and friends; where they develop ideas; where they ponder their memories; where they pray and where they die. The important things in the beginning are never public. Whatever comes to fruition in public was always begun in private, whether it is a person or an idea.

Though the physical movement of my life has been geographically limited, there has been a pattern. As much as anything, my life has taken its shape from the fact of living on the Ohio River. When one lives on a river like the Ohio, one of the world's great rivers, one's life bears the mark of that precondition.

The time of my husband and me on the river coincides with our marriage, which means also my adult life; we have always lived where, if we wanted, we could see the river every day.

The movement of our life, as well, has followed the river, except that instead of flowing downstream to the mouth, we have traveled upstream toward the source. Rather than collecting ever more debris in our current, as the river does when it flows downstream, I hope that as we have moved upriver we have been shedding superfluities and avoiding diversions from the mainstream. Traveling downstream is easy; one flows with the current. Going upstream is harder; it means going lighter, throwing aside excess cargo.

Almost any river has a pleasantness about it, but a river such as the Ohio attracts irresistibly. A river, unlike an ocean, bears a human imprint; it has a distinct personality. Like the human face, it is individual and unique. An ocean ebbs and flows, but a river is going somewhere. Like the human person, a river strains toward its destination, cutting a course all its own, yet ever flowing toward an end into which all rivers run. A river, too, like a person, is always bound to history. With a beginning and an end, a river, like a human life, runs a course to a destination. Yet also like a human life, once begun, though it may change course or come close to drying up, it never dies. Like the waters of grace that send the human spirit flowing into eternity, a river continually trickles anew from its source.

Riveted to history, a river concentrates our interest more than an ocean. That is the impression, at least, of a landlocked inlander. The aura of humanity lingers about it—for ordinarily it has carried countless people toward every kind of destiny. One can never stand on the bank of the Ohio without recalling one's own ancestors, this cloud of witnesses who flowed past this very spot. A comfort, these witnesses, strangers and nomads on earth, in search of their real homeland. They were weak people who were given strength, all heroes of faith, doubtless afraid, and yet they held to their purpose "like a man who could see the Invisible". One can never live near the river without sensing the link between generations. The river never allows one to live in a time capsule. It is on its way, and those who live near it are on their way, too, pilgrims to their homeland.

Being on a river likewise varies according to the personality of the river itself. It can inspire a holiday, as in punting on a tiny, gentle stream like the Cam. Or it can be a terrifying journey into a black unknown—as in one of Conrad's travels up the Congo into the heart of darkness. But a journey on the Ohio is like neither of these—neither gentle, because the river is a force to be reckoned with, nor terrifying, because it has been known to men for centuries.

The Ohio has a personality unlike that of a sprawling, lazy river of the eastern Tidewater, which is more like an arm of the sea than a river; the Ohio is unlike a wild western river hurtling through tight canyons; and it is unlike the Mississippi, so huge it often does not know its own banks. The Ohio is wide, definite, firmly moving. Viewed from the air, it forms an authoritative, defined path underlining the old Northwest Territory, making its way strongly to meet the Mississippi at Cairo—where from the air it really does look to be the dominant stream.

Unless one has lived as a newlywed on the banks of the Ohio, in a town with the charm of Newburgh, one may not have known the full spell of the river. Many of the small Ohio River towns on the northern bank between Pittsburgh and Cairo are historical and charming, their very names alive with classical or patriotic allusion—Marietta, Gallipolis, Aurora, Rising Sun, Vevay, Madison, Rome, Troy, Rockport, Old Shawneetown. Among these towns Newburgh holds its own. Although Madison is the loveliest example of a river town that is filled with beautifully preserved old homes of high quality, Newburgh ranks in that regard with Marietta and surely with Vevay. I have always marveled at the number of striking nineteenth-century homes in Newburgh—federal, Greek revival, Italianate. To have lived among these architectural and cultural treasures, to have visited in them many times, to have studied their history, to have discovered sometimes their satisfying order and sometimes their engaging idiosyncrasies, to have been conscious of the deep affiliation of these old houses with the past and with the river itself have been among the chief delights of my life. There was a time when our great hope was to live in one of these wonderful houses ourselves. And perhaps, had we stayed in Newburgh, we might eventually have done so. Young people have dreams, though, that do not have to be fulfilled in order for life to be rich. The historic old home was not to be part of our unfolding. Much to our surprise we hardly missed it, for another sort of home not only would fit our pocketbook but also would capture our fancy.

It was enough to be in Newburgh itself. Caroline Gordon, in her novel of Aleck Maury, has her hero say that there can be a place, not necessarily where he grew up, where a person feels completely at home, as if he and that place were made for each other. For Aleck Maury that place was the area around Merry Point, Kentucky. For me it is the small town set in the gently rolling hills of the Ohio Valley. Over the years I have learned something about myself. Though I lived the first twenty-three years of my life in a quiet old neighborhood in Indianapolis and though I have lived the last seventeen years of my life in a suburb of Cincinnati, I believe I am not by temperament suited either to urban or suburban life. Of course I have lived in both environments and been quite happy, and I would not want to live in a town that was not within reasonable distance of a city. Still, city life seems to me to be close and sometimes stifling. Suburban life seems rootless and without anchor in any larger community. In both I feel not quite myself. But in a small town I have been linked to the life of the community. There is a keen satisfaction in knowing everybody, in having all ages and races and classes living a stone's throw from each other and taking it for granted since it has been that way for generations. There is a comfort in worshiping in a parish that draws both farmers and businessmen. The unpretentiousness, the leisurely pace, the solid everydayness of a small town sustain and affirm life. The closeness of the countryside, too, always gave me a sense of well-being. To know that a three-minute drive or a ten-minute walk would take me into corn and soybean fields was to me a source of great freedom. Not to be bound too much to asphalt and concrete, to bureaucracies and traffic lights, is something to cherish. When I am out of touch with the countryside, I sense something amiss. Cooped up in a city for long, my spirits begin to sag. Some touch with the land is to me touch with reality.

Thinking back on those memories of Newburgh—the ever-present but comforting, unobtrusive neighbors, the teatimes and suppers with friends, the coffee chats in our cousin's big sunny kitchen, the Sunday afternoons strolling the riverbank and the little streets of the town, the Masses and picnics at church, the house tours and antique shows, the zoning battles at the town meeting, the Easter egg hunts on the hill, the collections of kindergartners we chauffeured in car pools, the spontaneous festivities on the riverbank when the *Delta Queen* stopped, the funny homemade parades, the cakes and pies we exchanged with each other, the drop-in company who never came to inspect—all these memories and more suggest to me that what Aristotle may have been thinking of as the polis, what he was describing, was not a city as we know it but a small town like Newburgh. Much as I thrived in my childhood surroundings—which, I now think, were so removed from the city around them as to be in effect a small town—and much as I now enjoy my life in a suburb of a city, I think there is in a good small town a humaneness; a sense of scale, order, and proportion; a civility that cannot be found so easily in either a city or a suburb. My tie to Newburgh has been therefore an abiding friendship. Its location on the Ohio River has made that friendship a love affair.

Our first home there, to which we came as newly-weds, was an apartment converted from a 150-year-old tobacco warehouse. It stood snugly against the pavement of Water Street, a narrow lane that hugged the riverbank. Early in the century the interurban tracks ran along Water Street. On the side next to the river the skirting then had been wide enough to accommodate shops and warehouses. But the river, ruthless in its unrelenting pounding against the Indiana shore, had long since eaten away the ground that once had supported those warehouses. Now the farther side of the street dropped sharply to a bank strapped together by riprapping. The plot of ground across the street from our apartment had room only for a brick patio, fringed with shrubbery, ornamented with a dogwood, a mimosa tree, and a stone bench.

Our old building, with its eighteen-inch-thick walls, was comforting in its solidity. Though the radiators in our first-floor apartment leaked, we overlooked the drips—and sometimes the floods—in favor of the magnificent unobstructed view of the river both up and downstream. From our kitchen window we watched the sun rise; from the little study we watched it set. Looking upriver, we saw the longest straight stretch of stream between Louisville and Newburgh. Downriver, the waters curled in a bend against the Kentucky shore, and then, out of sight, they looped back in a horseshoe at Evansville.

Our first winter there was a revelation to a city girl. I confronted loneliness—for nothing feels lonelier than living with the starkness of a gray winter river, where often the best sign of life is a gull or two, an odd sight on an inland river.

Yet I learned to love the winter river almost better than the river of any other season. That bare unadorned landscape, stripped clean of the least cottonwood leaf or the merest hint of green to flesh out the brown brambles tumbling along the bank, presented a world pruned to its essence. The winter river was the river that was most itself.

When the water rose high, dragging whole trees and even pieces of old barns in its fierce current, gulls and purple grackles, poker-faced, looking straight ahead, perched aboard the trash, piloting their vessels to their destiny. When the river iced over beneath a dazzling blue sub-zero sky, the spray froze in midair above the dam, and the waves below it stopped in startled suspension.

The winter river was a river that worked. Without the pleasure craft of summer, the winter Ohio was a river of towboats, of crews manning the barges in bitter cold, isolation, and danger. The men on the tows were going on a journey. They were men with a mission; they were carrying chemicals or coal or gravel

to their destination upriver at Cincinnati or Wheeling
or Pittsburgh. In high water the tows did not need to
use the channel along the Indiana shore; they could
save time by cutting around the bends on the Kentucky side. Thus in high water the tows were farther
away; their engines rumbled more distantly, and the
winter river looked lonelier than ever. That very
starkness gave rise to the most haunting scenes on the
river. In the dusk of a crystalline January afternoon I
could stand shivering on the frozen bank, watching a
brilliant purple-pink sunset fade into lavender. At that
instant, if I were lucky, a towboat would round the
bend, piercing its lone light through the fast-
gathering darkness, a heartbreaking sign of humanity
toiling toward a home not in this world. From far
across the water the laboring, surging hum of the
towboat engine drifted toward me, its rhythmic heav-
ing, its heavy working motor etched so indelibly in
my head that it formed the backdrop of sound of all
our Newburgh years.

As the year moved into leaden March days, the
river churned in angry mud whorls, leaping high in
its steep Newburgh banks, rushing mercilessly over
its low Kentucky barrier, spilling into Kentucky
cornfields to become a vast sea far unto the distant
gray hills that finally hulked against it. A single barn
stood sentinel on the far flooded shore, watching for
a hovering dove to still the waters. I always won-

dered who owned that solitary barn; I never found out.

Before long, while sitting at my desk in the little study, I noticed that it was spring; the herald was always Jimmy Cox's willow tree, which turned bright yellow weeks before any other trees began to show green buds. Soon the crabapple trees in the vacant lot next door burst into gorgeous bloom. Then all around Newburgh azaleas came forth, and finally rhododendron. Most of Indiana has winters far too rough for azaleas and rhododendron to thrive, but Newburgh and the rest of the southwestern toe of Indiana along the river in many respects face south. Azaleas and rhododendron do well in that one pocket of the state.

The *Delta Queen* began her voyages in the spring. Though now there are others, she was then the only passenger sternwheeler left on any inland river. We fell in love with her, marking our year by her first voyage in the spring and her last in October. She was pure nostalgia, and yet she was as real as her shiny paint and her red paddlewheel. Her marvelous deep, throaty whistle never failed to evoke a thrill; her calliope, steaming her theme song, never grew old. Once or twice she even docked for several hours at the very bank in front of our apartment.

As summer came on, the mimosa on the patio across the street burst into pink feathers of such tantalizing,

seductive sweetness that neither we nor the hummingbirds could stay away from it. Engulfed in that thick fragrance, we sat at night on the stone patio bench, listening to the men on the towboats talking as they waited to lock through the dam. Mark Twain knew how voices travel across a river at night. We, too, learned how the river mates with sound. Water so magnifies sound that when voices scudded across the still surface, we could hear almost whole conversations. One's sense of hearing leaps to life at night on the river. The veiled murmurs and clinking of dishes from the towboat cabins, the chuckles and snatches of talk from a crewman leaning in an open cabin doorway, the rattling of chains and creaking of ropes on the barges are so close and immediate that night on the river seems the time of most activity and acuity. For me night on the river is the best time, the time of harmony with our mystery. The only place better to be at night than sitting on the riverbank is on a riverboat. I have been on the *Delta Queen* and the *Mississippi Queen* when nearly all passengers but me were asleep. I have sat outside on the little veranda of our quarters, listening to the quiet. In the stillness there is only a low hum of the motor and a gentle sloshing of water over the paddlewheel. I sit for a long time, watching the sweeps of light from the big beam trained on the bank and on the channel markers ahead. The captain and crew never sleep.

Steam is the essence of midsummer in the Ohio Valley. By ten o'clock in the morning the atmosphere outside our apartment was so thick we could cut it. Humidity hung over the river in a blue veil, oppressive, weighting us down in a sluggish, breathless dampness. If we lingered long outside on those broiling July evenings, mosquitoes chewed us alive. They drove us indoors, where we were lulled to sleep by the surge of engines as the tows angled their barges into the lock chamber.

By late September the Ohio Valley took on the snap, the vigor, the clarity of autumn. With the opaque fog of humidity now vanished from the river, we could remember again how far upstream we could see. On the far shore the Kentucky farmlands glinted in the golden light. Sun danced from the roof of the lone barn.

As we moved into house tour time, the town dressed up. We set out crysanthemums in pots beside our entryway and, like everyone else, hung Indian corn on our front door. From our local apple orchard we brought home late McIntoshes, Ida Reds, and Jonathans. Though I never knew how to cook before I was married, almost the first thing I learned as a newlywed was how to bake pies, and apple pie was the best.

Our apartment was an idyllic honeymoon spot. We conceived a book and a baby there; we entertained endless company; we began to build a nest; we bought the first of our furniture, settled our tastes. We learned about hurt feelings and tears and making up. What were the tears about, I wonder now. Nothing at all, I think—only newness.

I took a step there, too, in that little apartment. One Sunday in July I left behind a childhood faith to take on another faith. I had little idea at the time what the step meant; my catechetical instruction, even though conducted by a solid and faithful Benedictine monk, had been unstructured and incomplete. Yet I knew enough to suppose that I was walking toward a more mature belief. Until that moment I had lived on the hither side of a veil, skimpily nourished by a thin gruel of faith that was composed of watery content and limp liturgy. Through the veil I could glimpse the rich table of a faith far more satisfying, a seven-course banquet rooted in reality and history, reflected in centuries of literature and art. I had spent quite a few years of my young life peering through that veil, longing for the banquet, almost without realizing that I wanted it. When I tired of merely peering and not eating, I asked to have the veil pulled aside so that I might step through. Though I would like to say that once on the other side I was overcome with the force of a dazzling revelation of truth, such was not the case. I only began to see how much I had to learn. All the intervening years since that time I have spent catching up, studying, reflecting, praying, learning what I did on that July Sunday. But perhaps my way was simply the ordinary human way of doing things. Much as we may try to consider ahead of time, there is no way we can visualize what our biggest choices and actions will mean— a school, a job, a marriage, a baby, a faith. We think we consider, and we do try to. Then we leap—and spend the rest of our lives reflecting, sometimes marveling, over the results. On that Sunday in July I at least knew enough to realize that next to my being born to my parents, and marrying the man I had, and having future children with him, my step in faith was the most important of my life.

Quite suddenly, as if someone had set off an alarm clock, our apartment, which we had loved, now seemed stiflingly small. We were expecting a baby, and we felt cramped, restricted. We began searching in earnest for a house—in Newburgh. We found our house, finally, our modest, white, two-story Darby Hills house. It was our romanticized house, our perfect house—perfect because it was our bid for permanence, our mark upon the landscape. And it was only a short walk north of the river.

Nestled in a tall clump of pines and assorted maples, oaks, and box elders; protected by a steep ravine and a creek running behind the property; graced in spring by bluebells and daffodils blooming along the creek bank, our house became a visible sign and seal for us that we had linked our lives to the eternal company of the race. Accepting the ancient duty of bringing forth one more generation, we went about the business of founding a family. If there had been any tentative thoughts about our union when we lived in the Water Street apartment, they were now washed clean in a sea of laundry and drowned out by an uproarious baby banging his spoon on the tray of his high chair. We lived with little time and little money in the midst of cereal thrown overboard and Richard Scarry books strewn underfoot. We took our summer evening walks along the river not hand in hand as in newlywed days but accompanied by one child in a stroller and two others fighting over who would push it. Our lives became so immersed in everyday concreteness that our roots in our spot developed without effort. We were as attracted to our place as the warblers and grosbeaks that invariably found us in their migratory trips along the Mississippi Flyway. We felt ourselves riveted to our house, as our favorite beech tree was wedded to its position as overseer of our front yard.

Our family grew so entwined with our house that we assumed that our bond with it would be permanent. We had a dream of living there forever, building additions to the house, making it lovelier. Though we were not fooled by any false notions of its beauty, we were convinced it had a certain charm, and so we were positive we would never outgrow it. Nothing, then, could have come as a greater shock than the news that the demands of a husband's career would take us away from that house to another city altogether. For me it was a devastating blow. The knowledge that most families move several times did not make it easier. It was my first realization that we are only strangers and nomads on earth. We are meant to be so. Our longing is for a home where we can finally rest; yet that home is exactly what we can never have in this world. To remind me of that all the more, the year after we left a tornado whipping through the Ohio Valley leveled our noble beech tree as effortlessly as if it had been a matchstick.

No home is ever permanent; that is a fact of our incompleteness. But the felled beech tree is not the end of it. We are not left with nothing. In our incarnational, unfinished world, if we do not have everything, we still have something. When we move, we are weak people who are given strength. Even if we do not like to be, we have some ability to be nomads. Wherever we go, we still retain the ingredients to build a home. We take with us the essence of our private world—our thoughts, our loves, our fidelity, our faith.

When we moved, we did not make the dramatic change I had feared. We simply moved upriver to

Cincinnati. Although we would not be living on the river, the river would still be an everyday presence in our lives. It would still be the fixture we took for granted, by which we lived our seasons; it would be the changing, changeless thing, the dramatic, flowing, permanent thing. Still, our move set us farther upriver—toward the source. It demanded a sharper focus, a sterner discipline, a greater giving. If our new life were to be watered ever more efficiently by the source of running water and to bring us to more fruitfulness, it required something in us to be pruned away. The vine of our family toughened and strengthened in this pruning. Though the youngest shoot was but three years old, the vine grew more profusely, and its roots grew deeper.

Our journey upriver to Cincinnati sketched the third angle of my triangle. It laid a geometric order on my life, for a triangle naturally hangs together better than two points connected by a straight line. Inside a triangle there is something; there is content.

The river looked a little narrower at Cincinnati, but it was otherwise the same river. The Cincinnati painter Henry Farny, known most for his great paintings of western Indians, painted just before the turn of the century an uncharacteristic but beautiful watercolor and gouache scene called *Winter Morning on the Ohio*. In the foreground two men in a rowboat are paddling toward a sternwheel tow that is pushing some barges downstream. Across the river on the snow-dusted Kentucky shore stand a farmhouse and outbuildings. The sun is rising above the far hills behind the farm. I know that farm. It is part of the winter mornings I loved years ago.

Chapter II

The Bed

There is a town in central Indiana, six miles south of Rushville, with the classical name of Homer. Only two features mark Homer with any distinction—a railroad track and a small furniture factory called The Sampler. For three generations this factory has been producing handcrafted, custom-made cherry furniture from trees timbered in southern Indiana.

On a September day thirty years ago my husband and I, newly engaged, drove to Homer to order a cherry bed. Much in love, glowing with lovers' complacency that our romance was unique in all the world, we were sure that our marriage would be grandly historic. As old-fashioned lovers we took two things for granted—first, we would not have a trial run, and, second, we would marry forever. We were serious lovers, therefore, in search of an emblem to suit a serious purpose. Naturally that solemn sign of married union had to be a bed.

The people at the Homer factory took us seriously. They accepted without a glimmer of amusement that we ought to have a bed noble, traditional, strong. They presented various headboard styles, posts, finials. With their help we chose, finally, a spare, clean design of simply cut headboard, the tallest pencil posts, and tulip finials. We were assured that our bed would be strong enough to last beyond us for generations of offspring. We were assured, too, that our bed would bear the mark of Homer furniture—not a glossy lacquered glaze but an oiled finish rubbed to a satin sheen, as satisfying to the touch as velvet upholstery or old leather bindings—but more than anything else like the smoothest human skin. Our bed was also to have the ultimate sign of a Homer piece: a brass nameplate fastened behind the headboard that read "Made especially for William and Anne Burleigh, November 28, 1964".

We stepped out of the factory into the glittering September heat not only pleased with ourselves but also surprised at the commitment we had just made to both a purchase and a life. It was still Hoosier summer; our bed would be ready after the leaves fell, just in time for our return from a Thanksgiving honeymoon. What we did not know that September was that we had just begun a long association with Indiana cherry furniture from Homer. The close grain and undulating pattern, the mellow warmth of cherry would become as familiar to us as anything in our lives, calling us away from the sophistication of mahogany or the modernity of teak, anchoring us firmly in an American and particularly Midwestern tradition. What we did not know, either, on that September day—although I think we glimpsed it—was that we had just signed ourselves over to a marriage in which the bed would be an institution. Though we had the fondest hopes of our bed being a place of delight, we had only the barest recognition then of its symbolism of the inner life of a marriage and the centerpiece of a home.

Even when people do not understand the full mystery of what they want to represent, they have a way of choosing symbols solemn enough to signify what they believe is important. Moreover, symbols taken seriously have astonishing power to confirm people in their belief. Thus, knowing somehow that concrete symbols stand for something more than themselves, we sensed that just any bed would not do, just as any wedding ring or any wedding veil would not do. We believed that a special bed, carefully chosen, unique to us, as strong and beautiful as the fidelity we expected to keep, might somehow help actualize a long, happy marriage itself.

Twenty eight hundred years ago another Homer— the poet this time—sang of a couple who believed the same thing. The man and woman were Odysseus and Penelope, as intelligent, graceful, and attractive a pair as any in Western literature. Odysseus was away from his wife for twenty years; the *Odyssey* is the story of his struggle to return to her. After his heroic service in the Trojan War, Odysseus set sail for his home of Ithaca. But Poseidon, the sea god, still bearing a grudge against Odysseus for poking out the eye of the god's son, the cyclops Polyphemos, caused Odysseus to encounter such rough seas and so many mishaps that it took the Greek hero ten years to get home to his wife and son. In the meantime Penelope, with the help of her noble son, Telemakhos, had been warding off the overtures of a hundred suitors, each of whom yearned not only for the beautiful wife of Odysseus but also for his lands and kingdom. Odysseus, arriving in Ithaca disguised as a beggar in tattered rags, revealed himself first to Telemakhos. Strengthened by Athena, the two men, father and son, devised a plan to slay the suitors. First, they managed to steal the suitors' arms. Then Penelope, who by this time had undoubtedly recognized the beggar but still did not acknowledge him, brought forth from an inner chamber the great hunting bow of Odysseus. Only Odysseus had ever been strong enough to pull the mighty bowstring of this staunch weapon, and now Odysseus, still in his rags, drew back the string and let fly an arrow through the suitors' midst. There followed a massacre in the hall, wherein Odysseus and Telemakhos killed every man.

Throughout the fight Penelope had been cast by the gods into a deep sleep. When she awoke to find the suitors slain and the announcement from her servant—Odysseus' childhood nurse—that the beggar was indeed her husband, she had a typical feminine reaction. She could not believe that the man she loved had finally come home to her. Even when she saw him bathed and dressed in fine clothes, she still could not admit to herself that this was Odysseus. Telemakhos questioned how she could sit so coldly staring at this man. But twenty years is a long separation, and she must have wanted to test Odysseus, who was sitting patiently opposite her. No doubt she was waiting also to be wooed. To determine whether her husband still treasured the deep secret that only the two of them shared, she set up the supreme test. Odysseus had built for the couple a special bed made from an olive tree, an extraordinary bed round which he then built the whole house. The scene in Robert Fitzgerald's translation when Odysseus more than passes Penelope's test deserves to be quoted:

"Make up his bed for him, Eurykeia", Penelope
    told the old servant.

"Place it outside the bedchamber my lord
built with his own hands. Pile the big bed
with fleeces, rugs, and sheets of purest linen."

With this she tried him to the breaking point,
and he turned on her in a flash raging:

"Woman, by heaven you've stung me now!
Who dared to move my bed?
No builder had the skill for that—unless
a god came down to turn the trick. No mortal
in his best days could budge it with a crowbar.
There is our pact and pledge, our secret sign,
built into that bed—my handiwork
and no one else's!
          An old trunk of olive
grew like a pillar on the building plot,
and I laid out our bedroom round that tree,
lined up the stone walls, built the walls and roof,
gave it a doorway and smooth-fitting doors.
Then I lopped off the silvery leaves and branches,
hewed and shaped that stump from the roots up
into a bedpost, drilled it, let it serve
as model for the rest. I planed them all,
inlaid them all with silver, gold and ivory,
and stretched a bed between—a pliant web
of oxhide thongs dyed crimson.
          There's our sign!
I know no more. Could someone else's hand
have sawn that trunk and dragged the frame
    away?"

Their secret! as she heard it told, her knees
grew tremulous and weak, her heart failed her.
With eyes brimming tears she ran to him,
throwing her arms around his neck, and kissed
　　him.

Thirty years ago, when my husband and I bought a bed made from a cherry tree, we were not thinking of Odysseus and Penelope, whose secret sign after twenty years was still to be a bed made from an olive tree. Yet the sign of a happy couple can be a bed—the bed that houses the secret life of their marriage.

The inner workings of a marriage are mysterious, something like the palm of a human hand. The palm of someone's hand is mostly a hidden thing. Though it is known to us, felt by us, as in a handshake or in the grasp of a friend's hand, it is, nonetheless, seldom altogether seen. In the normal gestures of conversation we may see the palm of another's hand turned this way or that, but usually we see only a partial view. We seldom see another's hand in the way that a mother opens her baby's hand and looks at the little palm, or as a man may take a woman's hand, turn it over, and look into it. Those are the gestures of lovers, of those who gaze upon what is personal and unique in the other.

As the palm is the fixed point of the hand, so a marriage has a fixed point. That point is fidelity.

We cannot live without a fixed point. If we do not have it, we go in constant search of it. Without it we are in disorder, and we cannot live without order. If we cannot have true order, we will devise a kind of false order just to save our sanity.

Having a fixed point means that we are trying to locate God. It is human to think of God as fixed, stable, permanent. To think otherwise would be to envision a god who was less than God.

Thus the fixed point of marriage is fidelity solidified in the concreteness of a vow, a vow that further has been publicly recognized by God and man in a wedding, a vow made manifest by a veil, a dress, a ring, a bed. It is in the nature of love to bind itself. Lovers always want to bind themselves to each other; in their urgency to have their love burst the finite limits of time and space they always are propelled to make, as Chesterton suggested in regard to vows, appointments with themselves for eternity. Even human love has so much of the infinite in it that the great drive of love is toward the forever, the inexhaustible, the limitless. The urge to be united sexually is only a small fraction of the far more basic desire of a man and woman in love to be together for eternity. For lovers a week, a month, a year will not do. Only the wild forever of eternity will satisfy their yearning to behold each other. To love with grandiose longing is entirely natural to mankind. It is the way in which we, unlike dogs and cats, are made. The bloodless, passionless way of modernity—that is, to love temporarily, to be together a day, a month, five years—is unnatural. Love strains toward permanence. The natural inclination of lovers is not only to proclaim their vows to each other but also to have their vows publicly and ritually acknowledged.

But if vows are natural, they are, as Chesterton said, also extraordinarily rash. What sane man, after all, seeing all the women in the world he could love, would swear to love and cherish just one single woman to the end of his days? Or what sane woman would give up the chance for more than one man so that she might cling to one? Only the insane, Chesterton would say—and that, of course, means lovers. Only lovers are daft enough to shackle themselves deliberately for a lifetime. Boldly do they swear their intention to love each other forever, to forswear all others. The danger is that the lovers may not be able to keep the appointment their vows require. Anyone can keep a vow for a week. But what about a lifetime? Even with their solemnly proclaimed intentions, can the lovers sustain their heroism? No, at least not by themselves. Thus vows have a superhuman dimension. Reaching toward eternity, vows are not only the lovers' promise to themselves but also their call to God to deliver courage and strength to be faithful. These vows, then, this great superhuman effort to break the walls of finitude, jettison the lovers into transcendence. Never, then, can they retract their oath that has called in God as their partner. Their pledge, recorded in heaven, can never lose its indelible transcendent character. Because they call upon God as a witness to their pledge, their words are not everyday words. Their words, signaling their intention to enter a covenant not only with each other but also with God, thus carry a weight, a reality beyond the representation of words spoken in an ordinary way. Their words are carried into the life of the Word of God himself. Vows bear a relation to Word that other words do not. As promises spoken in God's presence, they take on a power in their own right. They *are* what they express. They are so powerful that they convey to the one promising the vow the very strength to be faithful to the promised covenant.

Vows, then, concretize the fixed point of marriage, the faithfulness between husband and wife that, because God is faithful to us, links the married couple not only to each other but also to God. The Christian marriage is a trinity rather than a duet. Since God is their partner and their marriage is sealed in his life, the couple are saved from the crushing burden of carrying on by themselves. The source of their fidelity is outside themselves.

Fidelity in a marriage sets limits; it precludes other choices; but it also, in one of those great paradoxes, means enormous freedom. Whenever we make a choice, we naturally cut ourselves off from certain possibilities. Nonetheless, within the framework of the choice we *do* make, the possibilities usually are more than would fill a lifetime. Faithfulness gives a husband and wife the known, defined limits they need to get on with life. It sets the ground firmly beneath their feet so that at home, anyway, they can count on stability.

A man and woman who go to bed together every night, week after week, year after year, acquire comfortable habits. And habit, far from being dreary, can be one of the marvelous gifts bestowed on human nature. It eliminates the need for incessant choices and the exhausting task of continually starting from scratch.

Shall we go to sleep back to back, facing each other, or turned in the same direction, wrapped one around the other like spoons in a drawer? Such questions become shortly resolved by unspoken signals; there is no need to ask—one gives a nudge, and the other rolls over.

A wife who has looked up at the same angle of a husband's shoulder beside her every night for thirty years lives in a certain comfort. She who for thirty years has known the intimacy of this same man lives in a joyful sureness that saves her from the unsettling necessity of having to learn continually about a new man.

Fidelity created by the vows of marriage defines a man and woman. By setting limits, it tells them who they are; it announces to the world who they have decided to be. It binds them to one another so that they are freed from the perils of whim and fancy and the ebb and flow of emotion. It establishes sureness that what is here today will also be here tomorrow. This kind of taken-for-grantedness is the only ground upon which a family or a civilization can exist.

Yet the marriage vows do something more. These vows partially remove a man and woman from earthly time and thrust them into God's time. If vows are meant to be kept forever forward, then, in a way, they must extend backward as well. Even if we do not know it from the beginning, if we will one day take a vow either to a spouse or to Christ, then there must be some way in which we are bound to that vow from the beginning. A vow is a perpetual thing. It has a way of telescoping time, of bringing mortal time into God's own time. If it is the basis of fidelity and chastity after marriage or after holy orders, then it is likewise the basis of chastity before it. It is the logical basis, then, of the proscription against premarital and extramarital sex. If I will one day make a vow of fidelity to a husband, then, even though I have not yet met him, my vow is in effect from my beginning. If the smiling black-haired boy in Sister Maureen's first grade will one day ask the bald baby girl in the bassinet to marry him, then somehow all those years, even before they ever meet, they must have some claim of faithfulness on each other.

Fidelity, then, is the bedrock of a marriage. It is proclaimed by vows, instituted in a bed—cherry, olive wood, or otherwise. And this covenant of faithfulness frees us. But what is the freedom for?

At this point the secret life of a marriage swings into high gear. The real freedom of faithfulness is in letting us get on with discovering something of the meaning of the great Christian idea: the Incarnation. If fidelity is the pregiven principle, then discovery of incarnation becomes the absorbing activity of marriage. Incarnation is a truth that marriage is uniquely equipped to address.

Marriage is a way of life that by its very nature deals with concrete people; its concerns are not universals but particulars. I am not married to a man in general; I am married to a particular man with a name and a distinctive personality. I am not a wife as a general type but a particular woman with a personality who must get along with a man equally unique.

Incarnation must surely be the most difficult concept ever devised to break the human mind. Who was Jesus Christ—the God-Man who came into the world as a baby in the same way we all do, who suffered, sweated, grew afraid—genuinely, not simply as a charade? And who are we, personalities within bodies, who eat and sleep and reproduce and die like animals but who also give thanks and praise and pray like people and who love and think a little like God?

The question of our own incarnation—why we, who are not necessary at all to God, should exist at all—is the first puzzle. Then comes the second: Why we should exist in the form we do—as a man or a woman, having specific appearance, personality, talents, capacities, faults, coming from specific parents, living at a specific time in a specific place. The questions, of course, are finally unanswerable. Thus our response has to be, finally, not a quest for the origins of life but thanksgiving and praise in the midst of life.

As we grow older, our ideals become particularized. Great words like *freedom, love, goodness, truth, faith, honor*—words in which we gloried when we were twenty and in which we still glory—have begun to shed their abstract quality. Those concepts become ever more embodied in people, especially, in books, places, and all the events of our experience. Consequently, we learn what freedom is by experiencing and witnessing its use and abuse. We learn what love is by loving someone. The other person shows us what love is. Suddenly love far exceeds any abstraction we imagined.

It is fashionable these days to blur distinctions, to label people according to groups, to admit no differences between sexes, to press men and women into the same kinds of work. But to push this kind of equality to the choking point not only demolishes romance—to say the least—but also devastates truth itself. For incarnation is the opposite of equality and sameness. Its essence is particularity, differentiation, individuality, uniqueness. The response it engenders is wonder. Not only wonder but also the correlatives of wonder—astonishment, thanksgiving, delight, laughter. If fidelity in a marriage begets familiarity, comfort, habit, and permanence, then the incarnation of a marriage brings forth revelation, discovery, surprise, and humility caused simply by another person, who is ever new. In the space of one day in one marriage, a wife can take comfort in looking upon a husband working in old clothes, every wrinkle of his shirt, every strand of his thinning hair memorized by her—and then gaze in surprised delight at the same man dressed to go out, newly pressed, shined, and handsome. There must be no greater joy than to awaken suddenly in the middle of a January night, in a room made softly light by the reflection from a new snowfall, to look over at a sleeping husband, and then to be overcome with a sense of shock and wonder that this man exists, that I exist, that we ever came together, and that we exist in this bed at this moment.

Hence to gloss over the differences between people—especially between men and women—not only removes joy and romance and wonder but also deprives us of the possibility of making much sense out of the world. Even though sameness is in vogue—as boring and totalitarian a picture as if we all wore Mao jackets—the more accurate view of life must surely be to see mankind not as groups but as a collection of unique, dignified persons, each one given to the world as a gift—and to see men and women as distinct but profoundly complementary, needful of each other for completion of their being.

It is like God—the loving God whose nature is to give—to create a being that needs another, who can never live self-enclosed, whose nature, like that of his Creator, is to move out of himself to love another. The being that God freely created is a man and a woman, complete only together, necessary to each other on their path to the same end in God. Because love originates in God, the source of their love for each other is God, but as two particular, complementary kinds of human being, their ways of loving are different.

Though some may object to such an understanding of the nature of man and woman, I do think that a man loves first. That is not to say that a woman may not be fervently looking for him, and she may do everything to make it easy for him to love her. But physically, emotionally, even metaphysically, the man moves first. A woman may want a man to love her, yet if he does not make the decision to love her and step forth to claim her, there is really nothing she can do about it. As Father Francis Canavan has said about this natural polarity of the sexes, woman is the flame and man the moth that is attracted to it. When a man comes forth to love her, a woman accepts or rejects him. But if she accepts him, loves him in return, he may find that the waves of her love that wash over him are far more powerful than anything he hoped for. He will find, too, that the love she showers upon him is a buffer thrown round him, an insulation against the world.

A man in his love wants to be protective; a woman in her love yearns to be receptive. A man wants to come forward and hold her; she wants to be held by him. Every gesture of lovemaking confirms that pattern. At the richest level, a man's protective love means tenderness toward his wife; her receptive love means surrender to him. These ways of loving are the common experience of men and women who love each other. It was so with Odysseus, who struggled to return to his wife, Penelope, who waited for him. The protective tenderness of a man is not to be seen mistakenly as either a macho swagger or an effeminate sensitivity. Nor is the open receptivity of a woman to be seen as passivity. Receptivity is extraordinarily active. No one would describe the Blessed Mother, the perfectly receptive, accepting woman, as passive. Her openness to God's will cast her into total activity.

It is the great joy and wonder of incarnation that God in his goodness did not create us as unembodied spirits. He created us as people with bodies that have weight and substance. If our bodies may cause us problems, we also have the joy of loving with our bodies—of loving face to face, of being held by arms and touched by hands. In the marvelous incarnation of a marriage a man and woman making love are engaged not in frosting the cake but in the main event itself, an event as sustaining as Eucharist, as healing as penance.

The movement of their love—and lovers are never still—echoes the great swirl of motion that we can imagine God's inner life to be. We cannot think of the God we know as some motionless buddha. He is much more the kinetic God of Michelangelo's Sistine ceiling, where we see him in one scene hurtling forward to create the sun and then zooming around in the opposite direction. The loving God is in tremendous movement. Just so are the man and woman holding each other. Somehow, in mystery, this man and this woman are swept up into the inner life of God.

And behold! There is the greatest human incarnation: a baby. It is all one motion, one sweeping movement, from a man holding a woman to a woman holding a baby. It is all one sound—the sigh and gasp of a woman held at midnight, the groans of her labor at dawn, the tiny, furious "wah!" of an infant born at noon.

The nursing baby cuddled against his mother, flesh against flesh, warm skin against warm skin, his little round weight pulled close to her, is the amazing, unexplainable surprise result of her husband's flesh against hers, of his weight over her, new life from love and life in a bed.

The nursing baby is the wonder of incarnation in its sharpest evidence. No one knows why he is here or exactly when he began or who he will be. Yet here he is, thrust into the center of our life, drinking his mother's milk—milk made by her body but that she did not make. This milk is no airy, loving spirit that keeps her baby alive; it is food to see and touch and taste. This holding and feeding her baby are no mere projects of hers; they surpass any work she does. It is her participation in the heart of being she lives in but does not understand. What does she do, then, but hug her baby closer, look into his face—and laugh.

As the love of God becomes the incarnate Christ, so the love of this particular man and woman has become incarnate in the person of this cuddly, nursing infant. Because the love of this man and woman came to fruition in her womb, here is this hungry baby.

And so, at the very heart of their home, hidden in the deep recesses of their cherry or olive bed, hidden even inside herself, unseen by anyone, is the womb of the woman. Her womb, though utterly veiled, is a home within the home, the end place of love and the beginning place of life. Hidden, mysterious, her womb is the domestic center of gravity, which magnetizes her and her husband and their child.

If her womb is a home within a home, then woman herself is a home. She is an end for man. Because of the way she is made, because of her womb and her function as life bearer, a woman, in a way that a man is not, not only symbolizes but also *is* home. A home is distinctly feminine. It is not too much to say that there is no actual home without a woman in it. To have a home is a requirement for all of us. To find a spiritual home is our universal, lifelong quest as pilgrims. Although there are many beautiful images that mirror marriage and lovemaking, there is one particularly apt image for the act of love. When a man embraces his wife and finds his end in her, he is acting out our universal pilgrimage toward a spiritual home. He rests in his wife, and he is home.

Regardless of individual temperaments and dispositions, there is a difference in ways of being between man and woman that relates to their functions. Until a man brings his sperm to a woman, her fruitful womb is only *in potentia*. After new life is conceived there, woman waits for nine months to see the result. Thus, in a metaphysical sense man more reflects doing and woman reflects being. He is more activity, and she is more stillness. We sometimes say that women may be more patient than men. If they are, then perhaps it is that waiting is so much a part of a woman's being. The metaphysical difference between man and woman is evident from the basic questions each asks. Says the man, "What am I doing in this world? What am I doing to make the world go forward?" The woman asks, "Does he love me?"

Every home and family has its own rhythm. In its deepest sense that rhythm is that of woman's monthly cycle, the ebb and flow of an ovum coming to maturity, ready either to meet a sperm on the way to a receptive womb or to grow old and die, of a womb cycling round and round in its preparations to make an inviting home for a fertilized ovum. At the heart of a home, then, is the constant ebb and flow of a woman's fertility, of a womb naturally fertile and receptive and a lively egg looking for a mate, or a womb naturally infertile and an egg on the wane. The signs of her fertility are some of the most private and joyful mysteries a woman shares with her husband. A home—a permanent home—is an absolute prerequisite for her revelation to him of these mysterious evolving signs and for a leisurely, protected living in tune with them. The overflowing fullness, the extravagance that showers upon a woman each month in the time of her peak fertility seems a visible sign of grace that moves her, with Sarah, to laugh. Her delight is so deep that only her husband can begin to understand.

"Is this the way it was with Mary?" she wonders. "Does the Lord have so much fertility to spare that he wastes it all on me?"

Each day of a cycle is different; every day is a day when, if a woman and man engage in the marital embrace, they can anticipate a possible conception of new life from their own fertility or they know that they are naturally in a time of rest and will beget no child. Whatever restrictions they put on their potential procreation arise not from some artificial action but simply from observance of the woman's cycle. To intervene with some kind of barrier to their embrace—physical, chemical, or hormonal—would be the strangest sort of perversion of their love. Just as a man wants fully to know his wife, she wants him fully to know her. More than that, love is by nature fruitful; its nature is to expand. Hence the deepest desire of a man is to impregnate his wife. Her deepest desire is to be impregnated by him. This desire is something far deeper than what moderns think of as sexual desire, that is, in modern parlance, a desire for pleasure or for exerting power over another. On the contrary, people who love want their love to culminate in an end. They want a result, and children are their love made flesh. Men and women have vocations to be fathers and mothers. It is what they are meant to be—to be life givers and life bearers. The deepest desire of a man and woman in love is to see their love become incarnate in the awesome warm roundness of a baby. Perhaps that is why what is commonly thought of as sexual fulfillment comes most abundantly after a baby's birth, not before.

A baby is the incarnation of his parents' love. He is also their best teacher. Of all humans the most efficient and economical food gatherer, he gives his mother her final lesson on how intertwined she is with the concrete, in short, with bodies. She has learned much of that lesson from her husband, but her baby teaches her with even more finality. For nine months he has made his home in her womb. Ever since he greeted his mother with a faint little plucking sensation in the womb, as if he ever so slightly were tugging on a string, he has been passing signals to her. Now for many months he still will be joined bodily to her more often than not. With businesslike authority even the reddest, wrinkliest newborn nuzzles in, latches onto his mother's breast, and claims her attention for the rest of her life. In the economy of baby and mother a cry from him is often enough to bring forth in her breast the tingling sensation of milk letting down. The familiar pull of milk being drawn from her lives in her memory years after she has no more babies to suckle. A woman finds that her baby soon learns to entertain himself while he nurses. Without missing a single gulp he can smile, hum, laugh, play with his mother's face, or rivet his eyes 180 degrees toward his father or another child in the room. At night his favorite spot is most often cuddled against his mother, where he can eat anytime he wants and where he can feel the hand of his sleeping father curled around him. So closely joined to his mother is the baby that he is part of her fertility cycle. The more he suckles, the more extended may be her natural infertility.

A baby absorbs his mother's attention and time. From conception until he weans himself involves many months, even some years. It is a process—a pilgrimage, too, of sorts—that belongs in the home; it happens best and most comfortably there. Natural and elemental as her conditions are, and cause for rejoicing, nonetheless the pregnant and nursing woman retains a certain modesty that inclines her toward home. Everything goes better at home, away from public scrutiny and hectic bustle.

Gertrud von le Fort, in her book *The Eternal Woman*, spoke of a veil as part of a woman's character. Such things as First Communion veils, wedding veils, religious veils are therefore appropriate. The greatest things that happen to a woman happen behind a veil of privacy. The evolution of her fertility cycle, being loved and known by her husband, giving birth, nursing, nurturing, teaching children, making friends, caring for family and parents—plus all the watching, waiting, praying, and learning that are so fundamental to any woman's life—are all things that happen in private, at home, away from the public eye. The veil before a woman is part of her. Only God and her husband know what is behind it, and even her husband may never know it all. The veil signifies a woman's interiority. The interior life of a woman is her deepest life. Further, as Gertrud von le Fort said, it is an interiority that, no matter how intellectually brilliant the woman, originates in the fact of the womb, in its receptivity and openness to life.

Receptivity, openness, gentleness are a woman's proper responses to God's grace, particularly if she hopes to take Mary as her model. But these qualities are also vulnerable to assault in this life. A man for that reason senses instinctively that a woman needs at least some protection. He senses that behind the veil lies what is most precious in a woman. It is what he most wants; yet he also knows, especially if he is in love with her, that he must protect that very hidden receptivity. A man senses particularly how vulnerable a woman is who is pregnant or nursing. He knows that her attention is distracted to the care of her baby. Thus really and symbolically he protects her from predators. He is the guardian of the woman, of her womb, both as the potential and actual bearer of life and of the children born from her. As a guardian of the womb and its life, it would seem that a man would be repelled by the crime of abortion. Abortion is not only a violation of life, but also a violation of manhood. It is a violation of man's vocation as husband and father, which is the vocation of protector and provider, as Joseph was. In his role as provider for his family, in his work, a man acts as the modern counterpart to a primeval hunter. As a father-protector-provider a man comes to his greatest satisfaction and to his fullest maturity. As any woman knows, fatherhood calls forth his deepest and sweetest tenderness.

Knitting together the family of man, woman, and baby is love, a fidelity and common interest that is also friendship. The bond that draws a man and woman together in the first place is friendship. It is their friendship that they have decided is so profound and precious that they have pledged to show it in a way they will not to anyone else. It is their friendship that they deem so important that they ask the Lord to give them a lifetime of grace through the marriage sacrament to preserve it. The conjugal friendship, as the only kind of friendship that allows for a closeness so complete that one of its proper activities is to love the spouse with one's body, is the sole species of human friendship that has its own sacrament. The solemnity of a sacrament is the only befitting means to treat a friendship of this seriousness. For incarnate beings as we are, who are fusions of body and spirit, the act of loving another with one's body has enormous significance. Because our bodies are inseparable from our spirits, the act of loving with one's body invariably means that one's whole self—spirit, too—is involved. That is why casual sexual union is so demeaning and damaging. We are not people who can offer our bodies alone. Our spirits always tag along. Our incarnate nature gives us the possibility of loving another so completely that the love itself will become flesh in a new life. It is no wonder, then, that a phenomenon so powerful encompasses our whole selves, body, mind, heart, and soul. Moreover, it is right that a union that entails such complete self-giving should be exclusive. We can have a number of friends, but we can give ourselves completely only to one.

Giving oneself completely to another, that is, loving another with one's body, spelled out in the marriage sacrament—"with my body I thee wed"—means giving to our spouse all of our masculinity or femininity. Since our masculinity or femininity includes our fertility, then, when we love with our body, we are likewise presenting the other with the gift of our fertility. We can mutually agree sometimes to forgo this presentation of fertility. We are free to live according to the periodic fertility of the woman, for not only the fertile time but also the infertile time of the cycle is the gift of God's grace. If we love bodily in the fertile time, we can look forward to the glorious possibility of a baby. If we love bodily in the infertile time, we can rest in enjoyment of each other, knowing that natural infertility will preclude conception. Either way, both the fertility or infertility of the body and the act of loving with the body are gifts of God and gifts of the spouses to each other.

With this understanding a man and woman who love each other do not intervene with acts of contraception. Trying to love with one's body yet holding back part of the gift is no gift. It is a form of telling the other, "I love you, but I don't love you enough to give you all of myself. So I will do something else, perform another act outside of loving you, which will prevent you from having all of me." Most of us seem to know almost without being told that this is more lying than loving. It is simply the very nature of love to want to give all to the other. Most people, consequently, are revulsed by contraception. They want their love to come to its end, not to be cut short. Little wonder, then, that they turn to sterilization, even abortion, to avoid it.

To love another with one's body, to give all of oneself and to accept all from the other, including the gift of fertility; to see love through to the end; to accept the result of love, which may be being itself, that is, new life, requires absolutes—absolute fidelity, permanence, exclusivity. The openness to love and life that is the essence of loving with one's body requires a lifetime commitment with no strings attached, no ifs or buts. Loving without restriction to the point of accepting life as a consequence needs the shelter of permanence; it needs, too, the assurance that this happens with only one. God can be the only third party to this pair of lovers, and he, of course, is not simply the third party but also is the source of their love.

When a man and woman understand what they are about, contraception appears as an unthinkable blight. It closes down the openness and receptivity to each other that are essential to love. Thus it closes down a great deal of love itself. Because openness and receptivity are so much part of the very being of a woman, contraception is perhaps even more damaging to her than to a man. Contraception metaphysically turns woman, who is meant to be receptive and open, into someone closed, hard, pinched, cold—in other words, someone not herself. Traditionally, until well into this century, contraception was for prostitutes and mistresses, not for wives. Tolstoy's Anna was once a warm, open woman, full of life, albeit short on the virtues of reason and prudence. Yet when she went to live with Vronsky and became a contracepting woman, Tolstoy paints her as becoming fearful, hard, closed, and increasingly unbalanced. He wants us to see her contraception as part of the deadness that is destroying her.

Contraception not only harms openness and separates the intention of bodily love from its end, but it also endangers the exclusivity of love. If one could love with the body yet could hold something back, so that the act would never complete its end, then it might seem that it would be possible to have this sort of incomplete love with more than one. Complete love looks possible only with one, but incomplete love seems less valuable, hence not necessarily restricted to one. Contraception, separating means from end, turns bodily love into something ordinary and of little value. It cannot coexist with exclusive, all-out conjugal friendship.

In a subtle way, as well, contraception damages all other friendships. First, it hurts our friendship with our children; it tells them that sexual union can occur without responsibility for any result. Life itself is therefore devalued. Children begin to think, if their parents can have sex anytime they wish without accepting the consequences, why cannot they? Second, there is a way in which contraception harms our friendships even outside our family. If conjugal friendship is not seen as unique and exclusive, if it is viewed as a friendship within which we can withhold part of ourselves, then we put it on a level not much higher than other friendships. But then, ironically, all other of our friendships seem demeaned and less distinctive. In contrast, if conjugal friendship is exclusively, completely given to only our spouse, if it is seen as permanent and absolute and untouchable, as sacred to a realm all its own, then a sureness and strength arise between the spouses. Sure that their love in the body goes to only one, they have a freedom to have other friendships in their own proper sphere. Thus conjugal friendship, exclusive and permanent and open to life, strengthens our other friendships. Even more, it is the prism through which our other friendships pass. Conjugal friendship, the instrument of God's grace to the spouses, becomes the prism through which man and woman reflect God's love to their children, their friends, and the world. Love does move to expand, to grow, to be fruitful. Not only are the man and woman beneficiaries of the love of the other, but also their children and friends are beneficiaries of the light refracted through their prism.

There is a span of years, quiet, sheltered little-boy and little-girl years that a man and woman spend in preparation for their lives. This advent time, spent at home within the circle of their family, is just as important as the long expanse of adulthood. It is making ready for a long journey, a gathering of food, armament, and supplies. It requires study of navigation maps others have made before us, charts that will outline generally our direction but that do not reveal what the actual journey will look like.

A girl often makes her preparations in an odd sort of way. Thorough and conscientious, as girls are wont to be, she nonetheless may perform them as if she were asleep. Though she may look wide awake, she may be sleepwalking. But something eventually wakes her up to full attention. That something most often is a someone—a man. In lightning flashes of revelation she suddenly puts two and two together—or, more accurately, one and one. A day after the wedding she is an instant philosopher. And what has she discovered? Simply that God *is*. Perhaps she suspected it, but now she knows. From one effect, of a man she loves loving her, she knows that God exists. She now sees, as well, the most loving gift of mercy of a loving, merciful Father—that she has a partner for the journey, that she does not have to travel alone, that none of us indeed goes alone. As her love with her husband unfurls into the fruitfulness of new lives, she discovers, joyfully, that she will have even more companions on the journey. From a cherry bed have come a jovial, sensible little boy with blue-green eyes, who spends his life watching what makes both cars and people go; a gentle, sweet little girl with soft brown eyes, who lives serenely with her dolls, her books, and her friends; and a robust, laughing little girl with snappy brown eyes, who bounces and cuts up and commands everyone's attention. Could any woman conjure up ahead of time such a company of fellow travelers? Maybe, in the vaguest way, her husband, but her children, never.

Many years ago my grandmother remarked that whenever she looked on a newborn baby, tears sprang to her eyes. How strange, I thought. That never happens to me. Now my grandmother has been dead for more than two and a half decades. In her stead I look on newborn babies. Now it is I who cry.

The marriage bed in which these babies are conceived is the center where love becomes incarnate. The bed is the place in which to love, talk, plan, comfort, and someday die. Odysseus ended his journey home to Ithaca in his bed. For him, as for every man and woman in a marriage, a bed is central to the journey. It forms the whole character of the journey; it defines the way it will happen and who will appear to travel the journey up the river with us.

Chapter III

The Table

Stalks of aged goldenrod and teasel stood frozen stiff beside the roadside. Milkweed pods on rigid stems had long since split their casings, spilling seeds to the wind, leaving only whitened hollows. Rows of stubbled corn, bleached to gray-brown, sat in ice-puddled fields. Except for the black dots of crows and grackles in bare, distant treetops, the color of steel flattened an already horizontal landscape. The sky hung low over the winter earth.

At Homer, Indiana, ice glazed the only real street. Down at the corner a pickup truck and a station wagon had pulled up to a wood railing that marked where a curb should be. Behind the railing the little furniture store, The Sampler, was open for business. Though icicles dripped spikes from the eaves of the building, the steamy glass of the windows meant that within the shop tea was on and coffee perked in a big urn for the customers.

Inside, Emmett Newkirk stood behind the front

desk, writing up an order. From the little room to the right, stocked with boxes of tea, small kitchen gadgets, and bins of hard candy, there wafted a faint aroma of sassafras and cinnamon. To the left were the showrooms—first, two rooms of dining tables and cupboards; then a far room of living room pieces; and finally an upstairs full of bedsteads, chests, tables, armoires, and dressing tables.

After stamping slush from our boots and taking up cups of tea, we browsed through each showroom. Though we had long since memorized each one, and some things—like The Sampler—never change, we still relished the comfort of admiring anew the same familiar pieces. The sight of the mellow, close-grained wood, the silkiness of its finish, never grew old.

With this visit, however, we intended more than a leisurely browse. We had come to rectify a mistake. On the face of it we had made no great error. We had simply bought the wrong dining room table. Several years before we had bought an oval mahogany Hepplewhite table from a good North Carolina manufacturer. Everyone admired our table, and it was a beautiful table by nearly any standard. We admired it, too; we told each other we were delighted with it. But inwardly we doubted.

Then we admitted out loud: our Hepplewhite phase was all wrong—a vision of grandeur with pretensions far beyond our simple Newburgh house.

More bothersome, this table was an adaptation rather than a faithful reproduction. In my eyes it lacked historical roots. Unable to afford the real thing and never imagining a day when we could, we had settled for an imitation, a dressed-up pretender. We had fallen into the trap of imagining we saw beauty in something that had no substance. Realizing our mistake, I could not get the table out of the house fast enough. I ran a classified ad and found a buyer in two days. We now were back to having supper on a cramped little walnut table, but at least our integrity was saved.

Then we bought a piece of furniture that, after our cherry bed from Homer, set the pattern for our lives. Our friend Adah, who sold country antiques from her house in Darby Hills, had a cherry New York china cupboard that she dated about 1834. It was a good, simple piece in fine condition, still with the old glass panes in the doors. Every day or so I walked up the hill with our children, had a cup of tea with Adah while the children played with the cat, and looked longingly at the china cupboard. One morning, after what seemed an eternity of scrimping, I hurried to Adah's door and announced, "Adah, Bill and I think we finally can get the cupboard." I did not tell her that to hasten the scrimping we had cashed in an insurance policy that I had had since I was a child.

The cupboard came home to our dining room. Then we knew. Living in a small town on the Ohio

River in Indiana, we belonged with country furniture, not with primitives but certainly with pieces bearing the simplicity and straightforwardness of having been crafted a century before in the Midwest. Or if not country antiques, then good current country cabinetmakers. If we did not have the money to buy these country pieces, we would do without until we did. No more fake substitutes that pretended to eighteenth-century Georgian grandeur. It had been a mistake to try to transplant to the Ohio Valley a Rhode Island finery we could not possibly duplicate and that belonged genuinely only to Rhode Island, not to the Ohio Valley.

It was some time before we could afford a Homer replacement table for our Hepplewhite mistake, but by cutting back here, juggling there, we managed to save the necessary funds. And so, on that winter day at The Sampler, we chose our dropleaf table. This time we did not make a mistake. We were as sure of it as we had been of our cherry bed. The table was to have handsome spindle legs, an apron drop, an extension of leaves to seat a dozen people. Although our table would not be ready for several months, we were patient. People wait for what they love.

After that dining room table, which was such an immediate comfortable fit in our house, in our lives, we bought other Homer pieces —a big round table for the kitchen, Pennsylvania spindle beds for the girls, a graceful and roomy desk. Some possessions in a family are ordinary and replaceable or expendable. Others—certain furniture, jewelry, china, silver, linens, books, a fine Belgian Browning shotgun—are emblems of a family, each attached to a particular moment, giver, or incident of family history, each passed down from mother to daughter, from father to son.

Jewelry, for example—a strand of wedding pearls, a gold cross brought by a fifteen-year-old son from Crete, an anniversary cameo from Rome—is a special emblem. The most personal of possessions, it can commemorate our highest moments, watersheds of a life—births, graduations, engagements, weddings, anniversaries. Of all possessions jewelry has the greatest possibility for symbolism of the sacred. Little wonder, then, that in any museum antique jewelry is displayed next to the chalices, rosaries, pectoral crosses, and accoutrements of religious life.

Furniture, too, can be symbolic. Of all the equipment of a home, nothing indicates more than the furniture what the occupants hold dear and what they want their life to be. Most of the time furniture tells more than books do about who lives in the house. The furniture alone does not tell a story, however. It works hand in hand with the color and design of the room that surrounds it and the house that encompasses it. Still, the furniture is primary. Even before the room, most people begin with at least one or two pieces of furniture. For us moderns furniture has some of the security that a fortress must have had for the ancients. I cannot speak for chrome and glass, but wood has an air of solidity, substance, even protection. Moreover, it ages well. It spans generations. It is possible, of course, for furniture to be mainly an accumulation and not symbolic of anything but acquisitiveness, but the pieces that we value most are highly symbolic, closely attached to our incarnation. Furniture that we continually touch is our favorite—what we sleep in, eat on, sit in, write on, work on. No concrete object more defines our immediate world than our furniture.

Our furniture pieces my husband and I have loved are first our bed, then our table, and then our desk. We love them in order of both chronology and importance. One has led to the other. First came the bed, foundation place of a marriage, where vows were cemented, fidelity incarnated in new lives. Then came the table, the gathering place for a growing family. The bed means vows and fidelity. The table means fruitfulness. Because of the bed, there is a table. Because a man and woman have loved each other in a bed, there are faces around a table. Because there were vows, a decision, in other words, for fidelity, vows given life in a bed, there is the fruitfulness of life incarnated around a table. There is a further life as

well that flowers from the vow of a bed and the fruitfulness of a table, and that is the life of mind and
spirit that occurs at a desk.

Home is where all of these kinds of life grow—the
love of a man and woman for each other; the fruition
of their love, their children; and the intellectual, spiritual, and moral life of everyone in the family. No
place is so suited as a home to the flowering of these
basic elements of life. These most fundamental human
and humanizing activities belong within the protection of the home.

The family is the Lord's design. Thus it transcends
any political arrangement. Although the commonwealth or state is essential to the protection of the
family, and the family cannot survive without it, any
such political arrangement is merely a human construction. Hence, to serve and defend the family are
the purposes of the commonwealth. A well-ordered
commonwealth, by its proper arrangements, also
encourages virtue in its citizens. Today, however, our
world is dangerously inverted. Today the state, instead
of defending the home and encouraging virtue,
threatens the family in a hundred ominous ways, and
we are obliged to put up with its seemingly benign
but nonetheless predatory incursions. In this disordered inversion the tiniest and most innocent of lives
are under siege. Marauding barbarians who pillaged
the homes and villages of our ancestors were hardly

more threatening predators than the abusive modern state that first relieves a family of responsibility for its own care and then preys upon all the life within it. The modern state attacks first the most vulnerable members of a family; yet it does not ignore the strongest. It has become masterful, too, in depleting the moral and spiritual energies that traditionally have given families the wherewithal to resist. No one has understood better than Tocqueville how noiselessly, tirelessly, and insidiously the modern welfare state usurps control over families. Begetting, nurturing, and protecting children, the reasons for which a family exists, are functions that the state strains in every way to wrest from the family. To seize such control is the natural inclination of a disordered state. Thus the need for the home to retain its private character is all the more crucial. The very emblems of a family— jewelry, furniture, books, and so on—are signs that the life that goes on inside a home has a source and end that transcends the state. Life in a family surpasses politics. It is not the state that gives meaning to the family but the family that gives meaning to the state. And it is the state that exists for the family, not the family for the state.

Hence the vibrancy of any commonwealth comes only from the richness and depth of the private life within the family. Where love is strongest, where life is most closely guarded, where virtue is taught, where

moral values and traditions are an esteemed patrimony—that is, in a family—there is the greatest fullness of being to be found in mankind. No state can
approach, even remotely, the high degree of love,
friendship, trust, sacrifice, unselfishness, and intellectual, moral, and spiritual vigor that enlivens even the
smallest and most ordinary family. The friendship that
derives from the family is indeed what makes possible
the friendship among citizens in a healthy commonwealth. The family, the fundamental unit of and reason for all of society, is the driving energy of social
order. Thus the home, with its sacred, nonpublic character, is the nerve cell of the world. The importance
of a home is best revealed by one of the most astonishing facts of Scripture—that Jesus remained at home
for thirty years in preparation for only a three-year
public ministry. Even today thirty years is a long time
to remain in the nest. In our Lord's day it must have
been incredible.

The essence of a home is delicate, mysterious, and
mostly unseen by the outside world. The Book of
Psalms describes a happy man as one whose wife
dwells in the recesses of his home as a fruitful vine,
whose children are like olive plants around his table.
The truth of this image of a family still holds. A fruitful family is still to be prized as the greatest of God's
blessings.

The olive plants around the table are the very reason that the divine plan calls for man and woman to come together. Even though man and woman marry because, first of all, they love each other and, only secondly, because they want to have children, their fundamental purpose, whether they are aware of it or not, is to have children. The result of their love is meant to be an incarnation—a child. To say that the purpose of marriage is to bring forth children is not at all to downplay the essential love between husband and wife. Love is essential, and we know that from experience. The point is, rather, that this very love between the spouses far transcends the lovers, so much so that God uses it for a purpose the lovers cannot come close to imagining—the creation of a new being. This revelation of new life is something for which the spouses make themselves instruments but that in no way do they originate. Though man and woman make the stuff of their bodies available for God's use, the actual mysterious creation of life is the divine doing. Around the table sits the astonishing evidence that the greatest gift God can bestow, the greatest good, is being itself. My own experience is that parents never quite get used to the mystery of these new beings; parents remain ever amazed. It is a mystery—that from two mere humans, a man and woman, issues a family. Two in one flesh beget not a clone of themselves but an altogether new being, who has never before existed and who will now exist forever. From this new being will come other beings, likewise unrepeatable, who will also live forever.

I have heard it said that in today's world, when people live much longer than their ancestors, it is likely that a married couple will live together far beyond their reproductive years, and so the purpose of their marriage must eventually become unitive and no longer procreative. This view is shortsighted, I think. In the first place, it seems to me impossible to divide the unitive and procreative aspects of marriage. They are indivisible. Secondly, this view understands procreation too narrowly. Procreation is not simply the physical begetting of children. It surely means much more—the responsibility of parents not only for their children but also for ensuing generations. Scripture tells us to rejoice if we are able to see our children's children, and we are blessed indeed if we can see our great-grandchildren. Because the probability of our living to see our great-grandchildren is likely for us today, we have all the more reason to think of procreation as something of more far-reaching consequence than a single act. Ultimately procreation must mean the love, responsibility, and vision that link generations. We come to the table not only with those who are living but also with those who have come before us and those who will follow us. It is these family members, generation after generation, who symbolically sit around the table with us.

Thornton Wilder once wrote a play called *The Long Christmas Dinner.* Taking as his theme the bond between generations, he depicted the life of a family as one long banquet, a continual Christmas dinner in which the family members come in to dinner, sit and eat and talk, then gradually grow old. One by one a character rises and moves quietly out a rear door, just as another character comes in and takes his place at the table. Each character is unique. He has a purpose, a role to play in the drama at just the time he appears. Without him in the play there would be a missing link in God's providence, and the play could not go forward. Without him in his place no other characters could take their entrance cue; the action would stop.

Each character is here for a reason, a definite part in the dramatic scheme. Yet, at the same time that he is unique, and his mission is specific and unrepeatable, he stands also as a universal type in his relation to others. This man is a father like his father, a son like his son. This woman is a mother like her mother, a daughter like her daughter. No two people are fathers or sons, mothers or daughters in the same way, and yet in each generation there are husbands and wives, fathers and mothers, sons and daughters, brothers and sisters, aunts and uncles and cousins to stand in for those who have filled those roles in the last generation. When it is time for those presently on stage to leave, others will be waiting in the wings to be new fathers and mothers, sons and daughters.

Marriage is the institution in this drama that bridges the span between generations. It is the engine that God chose to move us along through history. By marriage are fathers linked to sons; by marriage are mothers linked to daughters. By marriage does a civilization make its perilous passage from one generation to another. In large measure this laborious passage through time is effected through the long Christmas dinner around the table, when one generation tells its stories to the next and that generation tells them to their children. What do these stories tell? Little things, mostly—discussions of who was related to whom, anecdotes of what we did when we were little, memories of how scared we were when so-and-so was sick, confessions of how we plotted with our brothers and sisters to get the better of Mom and Dad, recollections of what Mrs. Coe said in our second-grade class or Mr. Pence said in our freshman college English class, observations on an upcoming election or a current political issue, reports of a phone call from Grandma or a sister-in-law, praise for an especially good homily heard in church, comments about the food at hand—both pro and con. Small things—but over time, much time, they weave a pattern. Taken all together, through a lifetime of sitting at the table listening and talking, the stories become a tapestry like the long chronological embroidery at Bayeux—a record of what a family holds dear, of what its members will live and die for. Sitting around the table, the family receives the collective memory, runs it through the filter of the present generation, and passes it on to the next. Without that collective memory the tie of family members to each other, to their ancestors, to their descendants, to their roots in their community, whether that community be a church, a town, a region, or a nation, dwindles and fades. The collective memory stirs and keeps alive the piety that urges us to revere the natural authority of those who gave us being. This piety that the collective memory encourages reminds us to honor the advent people who made straight our paths, smoothed our mountains and valleys. It moves us to hold fast to the treasure they have bequeathed us lest we diminish the patrimony we hand on to our children. We, too, are appointed to be advent people for the generations we bring into the world.

No greater blow can be dealt to the collective memory than a marriage that breaks up and renders its children rootless. Yet, even when a family is derailed for a generation by a broken marriage, the resilience of a family, especially when it extends to include its wider membership of grandparents, aunts, uncles, and cousins, can be mightily profound. For broken marriages there often seems in God's providence to be a grandfather or grandmother or aunt who gathers up the children, takes responsibility, and tries to call forth the patrimony of memory that can keep those children anchored in the larger family, despite the disunion of their immediate parents. Such circumstances illustrate the immeasurable gift of being surrounded by an extended family of relations. In an immediate family births and deaths and all the in-between carry enormous impact, sometimes unbearably so. They stand out in the sharpest relief. But in the wider family births and deaths, comings and goings, trials and tribulations strike a cushion that softens their impact. Against the comforting backdrop of grandparents and cousins the large events of one's life, particularly the sad ones, stand out less starkly. It does make a difference when there are extended members of the family who step forward to share the burden.

When we in our family all gather around our table, I see us as we are now. I see my husband at the other end, the constant figure in my life, beaming because we are all together in what has become a special-occasion occurrence now that our children are in college and graduate school. I see our son, David, on his side of the table, firstborn, a big man, steady, reflective, possessed of judgment far beyond his years, his blue-green eyes by turns twinkling or serious. I see facing him on the other side of the table our older daughter, Catherine, serene and peaceful, in her young adulthood discovering how satisfying the intellectual and spiritual life can be. The sides of her long dark hair are caught up in a barrette, the rest waving gently on her shoulders; her brown eyes are soft and calm. I see next to her our younger daughter, Margaret, exuberant, generous, high-spirited, sometimes intense, her brown eyes sparkling, her dark hair woven into a long French braid. I see also, next to David, a new member of our family, his bride, Chris, a charming, radiant, hazel-eyed young woman, fun-loving, sunny, devout in faith and strong of heart, cherished instantly as one of our daughters. I marvel at how thoroughly she has captivated us and how naturally we have enfolded her, as if she somehow had been present with us all along. These grown-up children are not only our delight; they are also our friends. To our surprise, these friends hold dear what we hold dear. We are boundlessly grateful, for things do not necessarily happen this way. In the hands of these four friends the collective memory of the family, our particle of the patrimony of civilization, is safe for the present generation. We have reason to hope that at least from our hands to theirs the civilizational transfer has gone intact.

Sometimes around our table there are other family members without whom cannot imagine our family at all. My husband's mother: now ninety-six, an independent, dignified little woman of staunch faith, still with beautiful snowy, softly curling hair, her quiet good humor ever encouraging me and bearing with my idiosyncrasies as a daughter-in-law. My mother: youthful and active, loyal, generous, devoted, her pretty smile and girlish giggle as disarmingly a part of her as they surely were when she was ten. My father: distinguished; the doting grandfather; true patriarch; moral authority of the clan; leader not through force but through superior judgment, integrity, and vision; mentor in the intellectual formation of all of us.

The fourth grandparent, Pappy Joe, my husband's father, has been missing from the table for a decade and a half. Although Margaret recalls him only through story, David and Catherine remember him well, a bald, friendly man who prized order and who greeted everyone with a smile lit by crinkly, brown eyes and punctuated with a voice made gravelly by throat surgery. He had taken me in immediately as a daughter-in-law, assuming that anybody Billy chose as a wife should be unquestioned. During rose season I could count on Pappy Joe presenting me with a weekly bouquet from the supply he grew in his backyard.

When I look more closely around the table, I see us as we were years ago—David as a happy little boy in Sears Toughskin jeans, shoveling in his food, swinging his feet under the table. He has positioned a small Matchbox Chevrolet next to his glass of milk. Catherine is there in a puffed-sleeve red plaid dress, humming as she eats, secure with a miniature Fisher Price doll beside her plate. Margaret is in a high chair set on a plastic drop cloth at my end of the table. She is mashing pieces of carrot into her mouth and trying to make her brother and sister laugh. Bill, with more hair than now, is at the far end of the table, attempting to relate to me the events of his day but being continually interrupted by distractions at the table.

Then, as I look on, I see a brown-eyed little girl— something like Catherine, something like Margaret, but yet not like them. Instead of dark, shiny, straight hair, this little girl has dark, curly hair. It is I, Anne Husted, age eight, seated at the round oak table on Audubon Road, with my mother and father and my maternal grandparents, who live with us. My two-year-old brother, David, is clambering up and down off a window seat behind my father's chair. He is a fine, strong little fellow in short red pants. He has a perfectly round head and a sweet smile. I am exceptionally fond of him, but right now I am bored, and I think I am sleepy. My father and grandfather are talking politics, which I don't think is interesting at all. I hear them talking about President Truman. We have had pot roast and lima beans for supper, the work of my grandmother. My mother brings on the dessert, cherry cobbler. They always divide the work in the same way—my grandmother fixes the meat and vegetables, my mother the salad and dessert.

My grandmother laughs and delivers one of her funny, homely sayings. I never forget these sayings: that somebody is trying to make a silk purse out of a sow's ear, or that someone else is poor as Job's turkey, or that yet another doesn't have the manners of a louse or the sense God gave geese. My grandfather, too, has some expressions that I think are funny. He is always referring to somebody as an old skinflint, and he calls a bicycle a wheel. My grandfather is a handsome man, with chiseled, regular features; he is probably the best-looking member of our family. His deep-set dark-gray eyes always look kind, and he often smiles. He has awfully big ears, though, but perhaps they show up because he is thin. Grandpa has scarcely ever given me or anyone else a cross word. Even more than my mother he has the easy Walden gentleness. I wish my grandfather would hug me sometimes. I know he loves me, but I wish he would be more demonstrative. My grandmother, whom I call Gonga, says that Grandpa has chronic bronchitis and is afraid of giving people germs. Once Grandpa took me on an errand to the gas station in Irvington, our local shopping area. As we crossed the street and walked along the sidewalk, I reached up and took his hand. He in return squeezed my hand quite firmly and did not let go until we had arrived at our destination. All the while I skipped along, consumed with joy.

My grandmother is twelve years younger than my grandfather. She broke her engagement to a wealthy young farmer in order to marry Grandpa. I see my grandmother's animated face at the table, her gray eyes lively with mirth, her rimless glasses slipping partially down her nose. Unlike her friends, she has never cut her hair; she wears it, however, not in an elegant French twist but in a haphazard roll that she anchors at the back of her head with a few old-fashioned hairpins. Too unconscious of herself to be stylish, she has no time to spend primping. She wears matronly dresses that fit her overweight frame and black orthopedic oxfords that I love to clomp around in when she leaves them beside her bed. I cannot imagine a stylish grandmother. I cannot imagine that kind would be any fun. But Gonga is the most fun of anyone I know. Not only does she thrive in her role as matriarch and welcome everyone into the sympathetic warmth of her motherly sphere, but she also revels in being an entertainer, a comedienne, a cheerleader. When my parents go out for the evening, Gonga and I indulge in our favorite pastime. We prop up in pillows in her bed and look at the old Charles Dana Gibson books. She tells me stories of when she was a girl being reared by her maternal grandparents. She tells me how she rode in the buggy making house calls with her country doctor grandfather; how she volunteered to dress the dead infant next door for its funeral because the family was overcome with grief; how she listened through the door when her grandmother was ill and heard her aunts conferring on what would be done with "that child" if her grandmother should die; how a boy threw a snake into the boat she was in and she screamed and jumped out, even though she could not swim; how she ate too much at the young people's picnic and, to relieve her discomfort, ducked into the outhouse, unbuttoned her dress, stripped off her expensive new waist-cinching corset, and pitched it into the privy, bringing on a scolding by her grandmother, who pronounced her a glutton. I hear Gonga wind stories about our family tree. I hear tales of Aunt Nerve with her twelve children; of Uncle Bob, who came to stay with Gonga and Grandpa for two weeks and stayed twelve years; of my mother when she was two; of my mother when she was eight, like me, and got glasses, discovering that now she could see the flowers in the draperies. I hear Gonga tell of her sister-in-law, who is in her nineties, thirty years older than Gonga. I gather this sister-in-law, Aunt Anna, is our only rich relative, since she has always had a butler and a maid. She is a Catholic, too, which none of us is.

Sometimes I sense it is hard for my parents to live with Gonga and Grandpa. There is some harmless bickering between Gonga and my mother and my father that sometimes ruffles the peace, and yet the bickering ultimately does not mean much. My grandmother and my father, two strong personalities, never assert victory and have a deep affection for each other. For me the richness of three generations under one roof is the backbone of my childhood. My grandmother commands a completely child-centered household, where tidiness, timetables, and diversions outside the household are put aside in favor of caring for, doting on, listening to, making over my brother and me. In my view my friends who have no grandparents, especially no grandmother to color their days with the vivid primaries of her vivacity, are deprived indeed.

Once a year we have a visitor at our oak table. It is Mary, my father's mother. I have never called her Grandmother; she prefers being addressed by her name. Even though Mary is much prettier than Gonga, I do not like it much when Mary comes. I am intimidated by Mary. For one thing, she does not look like a grandmother. Rather than housedresses, she wears suits in her favorite deep red and flowing, long-sleeved blouses. She wears rouge and lipstick and fashions her auburn hair in little curls along her forehead. I do like to watch Mary—her graceful hands, her glowing skin that bears no wrinkles, her intense brown eyes, her radiant smile, and her dimples. When she is at the table, everyone else looks pale. But when she is at the table, I feel silly and stupid; I am tongue-tied. Mary is formal; she expects children to live up to standards. Those words "Will you play for me, dear?" send me into a terror. Only a hasty excuse by my mother can save me from revealing how dreadfully my piano playing suffers from long-neglected practice. When Mary asks to see my drawings, I fare a little better. Mary herself plays and paints. She teaches shorthand and typing at a business school. She is also a reader in the Christian Science church. She talks to my father about Mary Baker Eddy until he changes the subject. My father does not seem quite himself when Mary comes. Since he lived with her only until his parents' divorce when he was five, he really does not know her as a mother. Both my parents sit stiffly at the table. My mother is eager that my brother and I behave creditably. Only Gonga and Grandpa continue in their natural mode—my grandfather as his mild, courtly self, and my grandmother in her hospitable warmth. When Mary leaves, I am exhausted with good behavior. I usually throw a satisfying tantrum to clear the air.

Looking back at the scene years ago around the oak table on Audubon Road, I miss a character who should have been there—my father's father, Seth. I never met him. He died long before I was born. My father was but eleven when Seth, a young man of thirty-five, died in an automobile crash. I know Seth from his pictures; my father looks a great deal like him. Seth had a keen, direct gaze and the tall, straight forehead and long upper lip of the Husted men. He had dreams of owning a successful apple orchard but never made a go of his business. Had I known Seth, I would have liked him. Everyone did. My father's Aunt Ruth, Seth's youngest sister, said he was the most popular member of the family.

Seth and Mary were divided in life by a bitter divorce, yet I think that in death these grandparents of mine are somehow back together, reconciled in at least something of the bond that united them when he was the confident young man and she the beautiful curly-haired girl in my ancestral photo album. Although I never knew Seth and never felt close to Mary, I nonetheless am grateful for their having lived, married, and passed on their life to me. The Husted-Church union of my father's side produced a spicy mix of imaginative, artistic, visionary, bookish genes that complemented the thoroughly stable, placid gentleness of my mother's Walden-Hupp line. Had it not been for the touch of the flamboyant and unexpected in the Husted line, the family would be dull indeed. Had it not been for the solidity of the Walden contribution, the family would be incapable of laying down anchor.

Now the cloud of witnesses who preceded my four grandparents around the table are in their seats—

John and Martha Husted, Uzziel and Phoeba Church on my father's side; Elijah and Margaret Walden, John and Nora Hupp on my mother's side. The door at the rear of the stage continually opens to reveal earlier and earlier witnesses, whose names I know but about whom I know less and less— Nathan; Reuben junior and senior; David; Moses; Angell; and finally Robert, the first Husted in this country, who sailed from Weymouth, England, in 1635, settled at Mount Wollaston, south of Boston, and then moved in 1640 to Greenwich, Connecticut, where he was reported to have lived temporarily in a wigwam. On the other side of the water the identity of the witnesses fades out. The names fuzz into a generic Husted, which means "the place where there is a house", or housestead. My very name, then, signifies that I am to be rooted in a household. No wonder I am earthbound, loathe to leave my anointed, appointed place. I am not sure where the ancient witnesses lived in England—some definitely in Somerset, Dorset, and Norfolk, but also perhaps in Kent and the Isle of Wight. At some point those ancestors must recede into the past of the medieval yeoman and then of the Anglo-Saxon settler and finally of the Neolithic Stone Age primitive. Ignorant as I am of these witnesses, they yet gave me life, handing on through one marriage to the next, generation by generation, both the gene pool that would become specifically mine and the fragile thread of civilization that is common to us all.

As far as memory traces the names of the witnesses, there were no Catholics in the direct family line. Once, however, we were all Catholics, and so the step I took with my conversion reunited me with the faith of my ancestors. It is meet and proper that this should be—a restoration of order that had been broken for five centuries. When my brother, together with his wife and children, made the same move into the Church that I did, he sealed for our family the restoration for which I surely think the cloud of witnesses had been praying. The breaking of the bread around the table was once again united with the sacramental, sacrificial breaking of the Body of Christ in the Eucharist.

We are here, the catechism says, to love, honor, and serve God and thereby to save our souls and be happy with the Lord in heaven. More specific about our purpose we cannot be for certain. Our unique mission specifically given to each of us will be ever veiled in mystery, veiled because we can never see how our tiny role fits into God's total plan for salvation. One thing we do assume, however—our responsibility to each other, not only to those living but also to those who have died and those who are to come. We are to tend those in our care, our parents, our children, our grandchildren, our great-grandchildren.

In all this caring for those in our charge, we by a thousand and one tiny ministries exercise what is surely our mission as members of the human race— to pass on civilization. Passing on civilization means handing on the faith that vitalizes civilization, for no true civilization exists that is not the framework built around man's response to God's call at a given time in history. There simply is no real culture that is not at heart the outgrowth of worship and of how man sees himself in God's world. The civilization that grows laboriously out of the worship of God either remains rooted in faith or is dying. There is no in-between. Either we provide ways for our civilization to reflect the transcendent link between our everyday lives and the divine, or we hasten our civilization to a painful death from a secular bloodletting.

How faith and thus civilization are passed on is, of course, an enterprise of extraordinary delicacy. The passage is not guaranteed. Sometimes, even despite the best intentions, it does not take place. Certainly it does not take place simply by teaching children theology, although some basic doctrine is indispensable as the intellectual underpinning. It rather more takes place, I think, and as Professor Louise Cowan of the University of Dallas suggests, through the poetic imagination. Something must happen to fire a child's poetic and moral imagination. Something must so kindle his imagination that his faith becomes identical

with what he loves, and the Lord becomes the One he lives and dies for. The saints show us the power of imagination. Though their grasp of doctrine is impeccable, what makes the difference is the degree to which their imagination fires them to love the Lord and to give their all for him.

The firing of imagination happens often through reading the work of a great writer who was so inspired. It happens even more universally through the daily life of a family, in which the collective memory of the ancestors is passed on and enhanced through stories, admonitions, and observations round the table. These stories, taken collectively and over years, have the possibility of firing the poetic and moral imagination of new pilgrims in each generation, who must discover what is to be the goal of their journey. We are a communal race. The spark that kindles the imagination in one soul can catch fire in another. Another's words, whether we read them in a book or listen to them around a table, can inspire us with courage and a will to emulate the good that has so enthralled the imagination of our kinfolk, our friends.

Chapter IV

The Desk

I have great affection for the various desks in my life. The desk is nearly as important to me as the bed and the table; I surely would not have made my way into the Church without it. As the symbol of the intellectual underpinning of faith, the desk has been my pipeline to belief. My two desks—in the living room a cherry library table crafted at The Sampler at Homer and in the study a big Shaker trestle table fitted above with a cabinet for computer screen and trimmings—are my reminders that faith, if it is to last more than a day, requires the comforting bedrock of certain principles that the mind can grasp.

The desk in a household represents the convergence of the intellectual and spiritual life of the family. Together with the bed and the table it forms an indissoluble triad, the irrevocable merger of body, spirit, and mind. I rather think the bed is primary, simply because, as incarnate beings, we cannot do anything with our bodies that does not also affect our minds—

for good or ill. Because we are bodily people with minds, incarnated souls, fusions of body and spirit— the right order of the bed and the table, of love, sex, and procreation, leads to the right order of the desk, of mind and spirit. Proper understanding of the reality of our coming into existence is, in my view, a prerequisite for our correct intellectual and spiritual life. Our actions do determine the clarity of our intellect, and the more basic our actions, the more profoundly they affect our minds and souls. Thus, if we do not understand correctly the bed and the table, then we are blocked from real understanding of the great truths that tax our minds—that, for example, the one God is our Creator, that he is Lord of history, that he became flesh and dwelt among us, that his Spirit is with us in his Church. If we are wrong about how we ourselves properly came to be, then we will always find it immensely difficult to understand how the Word came to be flesh in the Incarnation. Many of those anguished and frustrated dissenting souls who proclaim themselves miserable under the authority of the Church owe their lack of peace, I am convinced, to their elementary mistake about sex. In turning aside properly ordered notions of sex, they have set themselves up to draw mistaken conclusions about the Incarnation and the Church. In separating body from mind and soul, they have caused themselves the greatest unhappiness.

The desk closes the triad of bed and table, weaving our intellectual and spiritual elements into the tapestry of the home. The desk can stand for both the intellectual and spiritual, for we cannot see where one stops and the other begins. Though we can speak separately of reason and faith, and we often do so, quite properly, when we study them, we yet have to realize that in so doing we engage in an academic discipline that ultimately ought not to allow us to divide the truth. Finally, there is not philosophical truth and theological truth; there is one truth. Only we men in our brokenness could try to separate it into a truth of reason and a truth of faith. Our pursuit of the highest life involves growth both in mind and in spirit. The two elements move along together. We know from experience that when we see something as true, it is true both to our reason and to our faith. If it were not true on both counts, then it would not be true at all. Thus we cannot separate our mind from our spirit any more than we can separate our intellectual-spiritual unity from our bodies. We are minds and spirits thinking and praying in our bodies. In other words, we are people who think and pray. Thus the desk is my symbol for the intellectual and spiritual component of our one indivisible life.

When we think about our intellectual and spiritual life, or what we might properly call our interior life, we find that we can look at it on one or two levels—

but then we can go no deeper. Although we can look back at choices we have made to build our interior life, what we see in this hindsight are the effects of these choices. What we cannot see is the point where God touches our souls. We can neither see nor feel God pouring his life into us. Where or how infinite meets finite is mysteriously veiled from our view. The deepest, most real part of us, where grace touches us, we know *about* but cannot know in itself. Though we can see the effects of God's grace in us, we do not know the secret of ourselves. We do not know God's reason for creating us—why he wants us here and wants us here now. For that revelation we will have to wait for the beatific vision.

In the meantime, as proof that God created us and lives in us we do have two solid pieces of evidence. First, we have the visible, tangible fact of ourselves, who obviously exist, along with the people and things around us. We know ourselves as concrete bodies, sitting at a desk writing, going about our work, driving the car, and so forth. Second, in addition to the fact of our existence, we have the stories of our lives. Each of us has his own narrative. I have a stack of old journals, a file of letters, a dribble of published writings—and my memory and the memory of others who remember me. Memory is essential to the kind of beings we are. Without it we could not remember that we are creatures of God who are pilgrims on the way back home to him. We are creatures in transit, people of the "not yet", viators, as Josef Pieper calls us. Because of our character as wayfarers through history, we must reflect on what has come before, else we have no clue about our future path. In its simplest yet most profound terms every life is a journey from and toward God. Why it is we must leave our home, so to speak, where in our mother's womb we were so securely in God's protection, only to be born and then to return again at death to God's complete safety, is a mystery. The purpose of all between birth and death is a mystery. But we must take this journey, which is partly a passage of purification and always requires our decision to make it a journey either toward or away from the Lord. Each person's life, then, is his story of the journey. For this reason each person's narrative is fascinating; each person's narrative is priceless.

Those of us who are bringing up children are ever concerned with how we are to transmit the highest values of our civilization to another generation. We know it is impossible to transmit our faith itself; faith must be grasped anew by each of us. Yet we can transmit some facts about our faith and our culture. We can, moreover, tell our stories, hoping that our own narrative will show our children that someone before them has loved the faith, moving our children in turn to love God. To say that we are people with memories and stories means that we are a historical people. We live in history. Within the limits of the choices God gives us we make history, as well. To say that we are people with memories and stories means, furthermore, that there is an objective reality to our lives. Our stories did happen. There are objective facts of our history that our minds did not fabricate. It is also true, of course, that when we reflect upon our lives, an interior activity that is symbolized by the desk, we are subjective. Yet even this subjective reflection tends toward objectivity. We sense that what happens in our lives has meaning beyond the events themselves. Their final meaning is decided in God's eternal time, not in our own human time. Thus when we reflect on the happenings of our lives, we try to discern a pattern, an order. And, admittedly, to see such a pattern in the great sweep of universal history is extremely difficult. In our own lives, however, we often detect such an order, sometimes even a startling one. It is then that we discover, much to our consolation, that a merciful God gives us ample opportunity not to change facts already accomplished but to make the most of them, even to bring some goodness out of unhappy events. It is the privilege of us wayfaring pilgrims to receive this freedom to reflect upon and to change our lives.

Long ago I began my journey into the Church—and it began in my parents' household. The desk was my boat for the journey, for the Audubon Road house, like all households, was a school. My father taught the big things; my mother taught the small, everyday ones. Reflections on God and man came from my father. "Smile at the people, Anne", came from my mother.

Although he did not know it, my father, a Methodist of sorts, set me forth on my journey toward the Catholic Church. He provided the books and inspired me to read them. The books and his attitude of reverence for what was in them were what left their mark—not a devotion of prayer as such but a piety toward what was greater, nobler, and more heroic than I, an attitude that I inherited from my father, that led me eventually to value the books as indispensable to spiritual reflection. The first books were those of childhood that my mother read to me and that I soon knew by heart—nursery rhymes, fairy tales, *The Restless Robin*, *Jane Elizabeth and the Turned Intos*, Robert McCloskey's *Make Way for Ducklings*, Robert Louis Stevenson's *A Child's Garden of Verses*. Then came the books that my father read to me— *Heidi*, *The Yearling*, *King of the Wind*, *Treasure Island*. I can remember just how with either my mother or my father I sat on the rose cane-backed sofa for these reading sessions. I almost remember what clothes my parents were wearing. I especially liked for my mother to wear her yellow eyelet-trimmed sundress with the matching bolero jacket. She had a pleasant fragrance of Elizabeth Arden face powder. My father smoked in those days; his clothes smelled of tobacco, but I never minded the odor.

I remember, too, how I worried that I could not read. It was an uncomfortable ignorance, not acutely painful, but still a thorn that kept me aware that I was not part of a world that grown-ups knew. Then—the breakthrough. At last I could read—not just "The dog ran to Jane" or "Tom went to visit Grandmother." I could really read. I was sick in bed with chicken pox. In one exhilarating moment, completing my second run-through of Augusta Stevenson's *Abe Lincoln: Frontier Boy*, I realized that the only word for which I had to call out to my mother, "What is this word?" had been b-a-c-o-n, not "backon" as I had thought, but bacon.

Bobbs-Merrill's Childhood of Famous Americans series, or what we called the silhouette books because of their illustrations, made a huge impact upon my primary school years. Over and over I read *Louisa Alcott: Girl of Old Boston*; *Daniel Boone: Boy Hunter*; *Tom Jefferson: A Boy in Colonial Days*; *Tom Edison: Boy Inventor*; *Martha Washington: Girl of Old Virginia*; *Ben Franklin: Printer's Boy*; *George Washington: Boy Leader*; and all the rest. When Jean Brown Wagoner, author of the silhouette books on Louisa Alcott, Jane Addams, Julia Ward Howe, and Martha Washington, came to visit our school, and I heard her spin tales about her famous subjects, I decided I would be a writer. I would begin right away. Some of what I began to write was pretty good, and that pleased me. Then again, to my humiliation, even I could tell that much of what I wrote was not very good and was not a bit grown-up. And so, except for school assignments, I took several years' leave of absence from writing. Even a child knows there is no sense in writing without something to write about.

The attraction of the silhouette books was, simply, the appeal of the hero—the hero set in the context, naturally, of a good story. There was no debunking in these books. The authors instead painted their characters as young people already exhibiting the traits of bravery, unselfishness, moral stamina, ingenuity, and vision that one day would make them leaders of their country. The young Washington and Lincoln and Edison of these books captured my moral imagination. They fired my sense of history as a grand drama sweeping through time, peopled by stout hearts who made the engine go. Nothing daunted that romantic sense until I grew up and encountered the sour taste of history as ideology and pseudoscience.

I moved rapidly into the Bobbsey Twins and then Nancy Drew, chaste, blue-eyed, blonde Nancy, with her pearls and sweater sets and blue roadster, collaborator in case-solving with her famous criminal lawyer father, Carson Drew. There were the Dana girls mysteries and the tales of Cherry Ames, nurse. These books were my light summer fare, good for reading with my friend Judy on her back porch after swimming lessons. They never eclipsed the stars of my childhood, the ones I preferred to read in solitude— Louisa May Alcott's *Little Women*, *Little Men*, *Jo's Boys*, *Eight Cousins*, *Rose in Bloom*, *Jack and Jill*, *An Old-Fashioned Girl* (the last the only fancy boxed book I ever received in childhood, a gift that to my glee I fished out of my father's suitcase after one of his business trips to New York). But *Little Women* was best of all. I read it at least half a dozen times and cried every time. Louisa's heroines, Meg, Jo, Beth, and Amy of *Little Women*; Polly of *An Old-Fashioned Girl*; and Rose of *Eight Cousins* were, like Louisa herself, upright New England girls, strong, modest, pure hearted, striving to live a John Bunyan sort of pilgrim's progress, following a path of virtue, simplicity, unselfishness, and Christian service that would gradually fine-tune their goodness and right thinking. Louisa wrote unabashedly to motivate her readers to high-minded heroism. She succeeded; if she did not always move the will of the young reader, she at least instilled the desire to live virtuously and nobly. More than one program for my own self-improvement arose from my enthusiasm for the good example of one of

Louisa's characters. Critics today undoubtedly dismiss Louisa Alcott as naïve, moralistically puritanical, and far removed from the fast-paced television-centered life of young people. But compared to the so-called relevant, "with-it" material currently published for young people, Louisa Alcott's world looks more real than ever. Besides, she knew how to tell a story.

In sixth grade or so I discovered the joys of biography. Because Queen Elizabeth I was a favorite historical figure, I became enthralled with the Tudor period. I loved nothing better than to rattle off to my mother and grandmother the six wives of Henry VIII. I even realized vaguely that before and after Henry, England was first Catholic and then Protestant. At least I knew the names of Wolsey and Cranmer.

Another favorite of mine about this time was the Jansons' *Story of Painting for Young People*, my first art book, which my father presented to me in his distinctive style of Christmas wrapping—a brown paper sack that always alerted me that a delectable book lay inside. In these days, too, I was reading historical novels, particularly those of Irving Stone. Even though I later lost my taste for that genre, finding real history thrilling in its own right, I was just at the age to absorb best through the novel the historical outline and flavor of an era.

By the time I was fourteen or so, my reading was taking a distinctly more serious turn. Only a small part of it was inspired at school. Although I loved my big public high school, was thoroughly enmeshed in its life, and had some excellent teachers there, school reinforced the impetus from home rather than the other way around. My father was a natural teacher. He had been immersed in the Civil War histories of Bruce Catton, Sandburg's Lincoln, and Douglas Southall Freeman's life of Robert E. Lee, causing the family to make a memorable journey to Gettysburg. I had no particular interest in Civil War battles, but my father's admiration for the high character of Lee and for the similarity between Lee and Washington stayed with me. I fondly remember the unmistakable presence of Lee at the campus of Washington and Lee University on our visit to Lexington, Virginia. Our pilgrimage to many of the national shrines—the old Boston State House, Concord Bridge, Independence Hall in Philadelphia, Valley Forge, the Jefferson and Lincoln Memorials in Washington, Mount Vernon, Arlington, Monticello—took on the character of homage to the heroes, without which I cannot imagine my growing up.

About the time I entered high school, my father's proclivities as an armchair philosopher were moving him in a new direction of reading. Book in hand, I had always been one to accost him on his trips back and forth across the lawn with his push mower as I insisted, "Daddy! I need to ask you about this thing

I'm reading." Hence, it was the natural consequence for me to trail right along after him in his new reading adventure.

It was the late fifties. The conservative movement, brought to birth by such people as a young William Buckley and Russell Kirk, fostered by others such as Henry Regnery, Leonard Read, Frank Chodorov, and Victor Milione, was in its infancy. Buckley launched *National Review*. Regnery and Kirk and David Collier began the scholarly journal *Modern Age*. Leonard Read had established the Foundation for Economic Education at Irvington-on-Hudson, New York. Chodorov started the Intercollegiate Society of Individualists, a title changed under Victor Milione's directorship to the Intercollegiate Studies Institute, a far more accurate name that reflected what the organization rapidly came to be—that is, distinctly more Aristotelian and Thomist than utilitarian and Humean in its view of freedom and society. Such institutions educated the first generation of conservatives in America. My father was among that generation; I tagged along. With the country still living in the residue of the New Deal, conservatism was unpopular. My father, however, was conservative by nature and upbringing. He was, moreover, a lifelong student who was strongly attracted to the grounding of conservative philosophy in Judaeo-Christian metaphysics, history, and culture. An Aristotelian Thomist without knowing it, he was most at home with a philosophy that looked to prudence, right order, and freedom tempered by moral law. The conservatism of the John Birch Society was not within my father's purview. His was a conservatism much more philosophical but yet always one of reason united with the faith of revelation.

One summer evening he gave me a little book, Henry Grady Weaver's *The Mainspring of Human Progress*, a simple explanation of the free market and its benefits for lifting mankind out of poverty. This unimposing volume was my first exposure to any sort of economic and political theory. I was captivated. Then I noticed another smallish book atop the pile beside my father's chair. It looked manageable; I browsed and then eagerly read the whole thing— Roscoe Pound's *The Development of Constitutional Guarantees of Liberty*. A dry title; yet even to this day I still think affectionately of that book as one of the most fascinating I ever read. It was my introduction to legal history and constitutional theory, my first inkling that the English common law and the Anglo-American constitutional documents offered us a rare and precious safety and freedom under law quite unmatched in any other tradition.

When I graduated from Thomas Carr Howe High School in 1959 and entered DePauw University that September, I was, along with the rest of the country, concluding a decade of relative calm. By the time I would graduate from college in 1963, however, the country would be sunk into the bleak, soulless seediness of hippies and flower children. The hippie world held no attraction for me; it was distasteful to those of us who valued soap and deodorant. I was hardly aware, in fact, in the rather bland liberal Protestant atmosphere of DePauw, that anything as countercultural as hippiedom was brewing outside. I was concerned primarily in my freshman year with finding something to cure my dreadful case of homesickness. A mere forty miles from home, I was nevertheless undone without the security of my cozy family cocoon.

Two professors, fortunately, partially relieved my low spirits that year. One was Fred Bergmann, a courtly professor of English literature. The other was Raymond Woodbury Pence, a bushy-eyebrowed octogenarian professor emeritus of English composition, whose greatest achievement, surely, was in proving to students that if they followed some simple but specific principles, they actually could learn to write. Dr. Pence insisted the craft of writing was no mystery; if one used practice and diligent application of principle, he could attain mature writing. Mastery, however, came at the cost of pain. Writing, said Dr. Pence, "is 1 percent inspiration and 99 percent perspiration". Pence was a disciplinarian and drill sergeant. Not only had he taught English, Latin, and physics, but also in his youth he had been a prize-fighter. He was tough; his aphorisms, anything but platitudes, were orders for his students: "It is not enough to write so that you can be understood; you must write so that you cannot possibly be *misunderstood*." "Avoid even a hint of monotony." "Tell them what you are going to tell them; then tell them; then tell them what you told them." One was lucky to see at the bottom of a composition the vigorous black scrawl: "This is too good not to be better" and horrified indeed to read in the middle of a paragraph the red ink death sentence: "I quit here!"

Dr. Pence was a teacher of composition; he discoursed very little on the nature of language, and yet his class was a year-long lecture on the reality of the word. The unspoken philosophy that underlay his approach to writing was reverence for the sanctity of words as reflective of the Word. For Pence the very nature of words was to mean something. If words and the way they were strung together in sentences and paragraphs did not accurately depict reality, then they meant nothing at all, and the student must begin again. Learning to write was precisely the lesson of using words in connection to reality. Words by their very nature have meaning, Pence taught, or they are not words; they are only inhuman babble. The very purpose of language is to be understood. If Dr. Pence had encountered the modern deconstructionists who assert that words mean nothing more than what the reader wants them to mean, he would have gone after them with his boxing gloves.

In addition to Bergmann and Pence, one other gift shed a glimmer of light during that dismal freshman year. That third gift was my discovery of ISI, the Intercollegiate Studies Institute. My acquaintance with ISI unquestionably directly relates to my becoming a Catholic. With the exception of my falling in love with and marrying a Catholic, I am convinced that no other single influence was as strong as ISI in my decision to leave Protestantism behind and join the Catholic Church. This was so despite the fact that ISI was not a Catholic organization and, indeed, had among its most active members some agnostic libertarians. It was so because ISI, specifically an educational, not a political, organization, not only aimed at teaching undergraduate and graduate students the theory of the twin pillars of liberty—limited constitutional government and free market economics—but also encouraged them to ask the question of ends, the question of why we are created free in the first place. What is our freedom for? To answer that question, one travels inevitably into the heart of the Judaeo-Christian classical and Biblical tradition and is likely to discover, as I did, that the convergence point of that tradition is the Catholic

Church, and its emanation is the Judaeo-Christian civilization that has touched every part of the globe. I was but one who saw the Church as especially conducive to fostering a civilization respectful of man, one that would value the delicate balance between freedom and law. Some of ISI's best lecturers and most stalwart members were Catholics or nearly so.

On a Sunday evening in the autumn of my freshman year I received a surprise visit from Don Lipsett, an Indianapolis acquaintance of my father and Midwest representative of the fledgling ISI. Though I had never heard of ISI, I listened to his hope that my friends and I would help put together an ISI chapter at DePauw. Who now but a tiny handful of us remembers that DePauw had an ISI chapter in the early sixties? Nonetheless, our little chapter, with its occasional speakers from the ISI lecture circuit, combined with the publications that ISI promoted and the conferences that ISI sponsored periodically in Indianapolis, its regional headquarters, were my great battery charges. Through one impoverished little organization that cared about the integrity of young people's minds, I and a generation of others like me on campuses around the country gained access to writers and speakers we otherwise would never have encountered. Russell Kirk, Richard Weaver, William Buckley, Stephen Tonsor, Gerhart Niemeyer, Erik von Kuehnelt-Leddihn, Frank Meyer, Brent Bozell,

Stanton Evans, Peter Stanlis, Benjamin Rogge all lectured in the early ISI days. Although others came later, these were among the earliest on the scene. Were it not for these and other hardy soldiers who lectured and wrote in order to teach young people what they could not hear on their almost universally liberal campuses, there would not be the pockets of second- and third-generation conservatives teaching on campuses today. I note with immense gratitude that a number of these ISI descendants are, interestingly enough, Catholics, some from the cradle, others through conversion. I believe that fact is more than coincidental.

The books were essential. Kirk's classic *The Conservative Mind* was hugely important to me; it was the first book I met that attempted to set the conservative movement in its broader historical setting and to trace its roots from Burke to Eliot. Thanks to that book, too, I gleaned my first clue that I would one day spend much time in studying and writing about John Adams. Forty years ago Russell Kirk insisted that the first principle of conservatism is recognition of an enduring moral order. Human nature is real and constant, and moral truths are permanent. Kirk taught, moreover, that order in the soul is indispensable to order in the commonwealth. Until his recent death, he was still so teaching, more profoundly than ever, as his *Roots of American Order* and *Politics of Pru-*

dence attest. For my own intellectual, spiritual, and moral formation Russell Kirk's writings have been of incalculable influence.

Inspired by Kirk's emphasis on Edmund Burke, I, too, read Burke's *Reflections on the Revolution in France* and found it to be a key book. Equally important were Peter Stanlis' works on Burke. My reading of Burke, Kirk, and Stanlis taught me the dangers of revolution, borne out by the thorough upheaval of the French Revolution, which grew out of the French Enlightenment. The American Revolution, in contrast to the French, was not a revolution. It was rather a conservation, a reformation, a restoration or calling back to first principles.

Nearly as important to me as Kirk was Richard Weaver, a teacher of rhetoric, philosophy, literature, and composition at the University of Chicago. I was enchanted with this shy little bulldog-faced man who revered both the word and the Word as much as my hero Dr. Pence. I loved his books *Ideas Have Consequences* and the *Ethics of Rhetoric* and especially his *Visions of Order*, all masterful analyses of the disintegration of modern culture. I was particularly fond of a little pamphlet he wrote on education. Influenced by the southern agrarians, Weaver also wrote a number of essays on the meaning of the South, which have been collected as the *Southern Essays*. Of that collection, "Lee the Philosopher" is surely one of the most beautiful essays ever written by anyone. Weaver, despite his southern frame of reference, greatly admired Lincoln. A remarkable essay on Lincoln's "Argument by Definition" is a highlight of the *Ethics of Rhetoric*. It always pleased me that in his southern emphasis on place, Weaver allowed that outside the South there was possibly one other locale in which the inhabitants considered themselves as belonging indelibly to their spot of earth—and that place was the land of the Indiana Hoosiers.

Hayek's *The Road to Serfdom* was on my shelf. I gained much, too, from Gottfried Dietze's *In Defense of Property* and *America's Political Dilemma*. I read Edmund Opitz' *Religion and Capitalism: Allies, Not Enemies* and Wilhelm Roepke's *The Humane Economy*. I made myself read some of Ludwig Von Mises. Just as important as the books—perhaps more so, because its influence has been sustained over three decades—was the journal *Modern Age*, the effort of Kirk, Regnery, and Collier to provide a serious, scholarly forum for conservative thinkers. *Modern Age* was mostly above my head; it aimed at graduate students and faculty. *The Intercollegiate Review*, published by ISI for undergraduates and containing both student and faculty authors, was just my speed. Serious but understandable, the *Review* gave me, other than my summer features and book reviews in *The Indianapolis Star*, my first bylines beyond school publications. The

Review laid deep roots. A number of authors currently teaching and writing or working in journalism, foundations, think tanks, or in law offices or government published first in *The Intercollegiate Review*.

When I look back over three decades and try to assess not only why ISI meant so much to us in that first generation of conservatives but also why, through the political, religious, and cultural wars of thirty years, it continues to influence young people, I believe that the answer must come from its insistence upon recognizing the moral and spiritual core of freedom. Political liberty and economic liberty are no liberty at all without basis in the inherent respect we must have for the transcendent end of man. Politics and economics do not explain the whole of man. Only God can explain man. Our end, then, does not rest with us. Politics and economics—such as Marxism—that claim to explain the whole of our existence must surely be false. ISI, it seems to me, has always understood that man's yearning is fundamentally religious and can never be satisfied either by Marxism, which would drown us in a collective society and make the collective will the final authority of truth, or by libertarianism, which would isolate us as atoms and make our own individual wills the ultimate terrifying authority.

The early years of the conservative movement were not only intellectually and spiritually challenging; they were also exciting and inspiring. There was a certain clandestine delight in claiming kinship with an unpopular, beleaguered, elite minority, to be reading books and journals that few other people on campus read. Youth thrives on heroism. In helping to fight the good fight, we fancied ourselves heroic. In our way, though quietly looking and acting like everyone else on campus, we were as countercultural to the prevailing mushy liberalism as the hippies who were mounting forces in the opposite direction. I like to think we were building civilization. They were destroying it. Indeed, they were an extreme outgrowth of liberalism's muddled brain—and so perhaps they were not so countercultural after all.

The ISI influence, when I was a young adult, was my first major impetus toward Catholicism. The second was about to swing into gear.

When I returned to DePauw for my sophomore year, much refreshed after a happy, productive summer working at *The Star* as a beginning reporter, I discovered a new world: history. DePauw had an excellent history department, especially European history. Dwight Ling and John Baughman, two of the best professors in the university, were dedicated, inspiring teachers who loved their subject; they were the sort of teachers who cause young people to wonder if they, too, ought to consider teaching. I soon enrolled in an independent study program in history, which freed me from most lecture courses in the department and allowed me to browse for hours in the library, to read and write, to spend precious time in seminars with a professor and with the little band of students who became close friends. Consecutively, as I took the courses and seminars, I fell in love first with ancient history, then the Middle Ages, then the Renaissance, then early modern Europe, then modern Europe. Tucked away in my carrel in the Roy O. West Library, I rejoiced in Edith Hamilton's *The Greek Way*, in H. D. F. Kitto's *The Greeks*, Basil Willey's *The Seventeenth Century Background*, W. H. Lewis' *The Splendid Century*, or Jacob Burckhardt's *The Civilization of the Renaissance in Italy*. On a drizzly March day I could look out on the students in khaki raincoats who filed in and out of the ramshackle little coffeehouse, The Duck, for their pick-me-up instant Nescafe and Saps' doughnut in plastic wrapper, and I was glad simply to be alive. I thought then and I think now that the years I spent in the independent history program were nearly idyllic, a rare, brief moment when we and our professors formed something very close to a community of scholars.

It happened that my favorite historical periods, the High Middle Ages and the Baroque, were also golden ages of the Church. The greatest names of the Catholic intellectual tradition thus were coming at least into my cursory acquaintance. Almost unrecognized by me, I was developing a quiet little romance with these names, an attraction enhanced by my new attendance on Sundays at the Episcopal church in Greencastle. If not the doctrine, the culture and the richness in the sacramental tradition of the Church were beginning to intrigue me. It was nearly impossible to study the Middle Ages, for example, without studying the Church. The Middle Ages *was* the Church. Just how Protestantism, which stemmed officially from the sixteenth century, and in an even more complicated fashion Methodism, which arose in the eighteenth century, might fit with the larger history of Europe before those centuries was becoming a troublesome problem, even an embarrassment to me. Moreover, looking into the history of Europe and consequently of the Church, it was evident that Catholicism had an ancient intellectual tradition and was not, as I had formerly thought, a superstition. Not only did it have an intellectual tradition, but also it was apparent that its tradition was so much the main stem that later fragmentations of it were either reactions to it or efforts to continue it.

Early in my senior year I was wondering what I would choose as a topic for my thesis. Sometime that fall, Erik von Kuehnelt-Leddihn, an Austrian writer, lecturer, and contributor to *National Review*, gave a lecture at DePauw under ISI auspices. In conversation after the lecture he told me of the Old Catholic

Church in Holland, which still existed as a descendant of the Jansenist heresy of the seventeenth century. Fascinated by the tale of heresy and political intrigue, I chose as my topic seventeenth-century Jansenism. I was a senior; we all had spring fever— and yet the greatest joys of my final undergraduate semester were the hours I spent researching and writing about Antoine Arnauld, Pascal, the nuns of Port Royal, Richelieu, Louis XIV, and the Jesuits. Rather to my surprise, at the conclusion of my prowls through the thickets of Gallicanism and monarchical absolutism, wrapped together with Pelagianism and Jansenism, I discovered that I sided with the Pope and the Jesuits.

The months of my Jansenism research were my introduction, as well, to a captivating author: Ronald Knox and his landmark book *Enthusiasm*. Monsignor Knox, himself a convert, described enthusiasm in sympathetic but finally critical terms, stressing that reason is a firmer underpinning of faith than emotion, leaving me with the distinct realization that I did not want to be an enthusiast and yet that I was caught in the predicament of facing Methodism as a form of enthusiasm.

By this time, intellectually at least, I was no longer a Methodist. I was no longer even a Protestant, though it had not occurred to me to make any further move while I was on campus than to attend the Episcopal church. At home I still went to the Methodist church with my parents. Nevertheless, in that intermediate stage of Episcopalianism I learned the tremendous difference between the Christian churches with a sacramental, liturgical tradition—Roman, Orthodox, Anglican, and Lutheran—and those in which the sermon is the centerpiece—Methodist, Presbyterian, Baptist, Evangelical, Congregational. Whether one's inclination toward one or the other depends more on disposition or on conviction I had no idea. Having experienced, however, the richness and beauty of the sacramental, liturgical type, I knew I could never settle for what seemed the emptiness of the other.

I had come to this point of my spiritual journey mostly through the desk. The people who had moved me toward the Catholic Church were those I had encountered in books. They sprang forth from history.

Concentrating my undergraduate attention on the study of history was, I think, a blessing of providence. History is a study exactly suited to the generalist who has some aptitude for description and synthesis but less for close abstraction. It is made to order for one who wants to know something about a great many things and wants to understand how various kinds of knowledge fit together in broad perspective but who grows impatient with narrowing the focus to one specialized niche. At nineteen or twenty I was too young to master the abstractions of philosophy and theology. Yet I wanted to know something of those disciplines; I found them fascinating. Through history, which is the story of all disciplines, I could learn something of philosophy, theology, literature, politics, art, all of which attracted me—and even something of science, which attracted me less but which I still enjoyed. In the study of history I could be happily a jack-of-all-trades, though master of none.

Truth is a unity. Because all genuine disciplines point to that unity, one can find truth in one discipline that will reflect the truth of the whole. Even though a general background in all disciplines is a prerequisite, most people eventually are drawn more to one or two disciplines than to the others. Some people have come to the Church through philosophy. But I did not have a truly philosophical mind, or at least it was undeveloped at that early stage. I instead came to the Church through history, which included by its very nature big doses of literature, politics, art, philosophy, theology. I came to the Church through the great dazzling tapestry in which over two thousand years all these disciplines had woven their truths. This huge rich cloth of the Church—which covered all of Judaeo-Christian civilization—was the only fabric vast enough to encompass my imagination, appear understandable to my mind, and capture my heart. That the doctrine of the Church was cloudy to me was not as important at that moment as its universality. The Church was the widest thing on earth I could think of. I could not give my heart to less.

The great English historian Lord Macaulay, scarcely a lover of the Roman Church, nonetheless recognized its immense unshakableness. At the beginning of a long, admiring, and eloquent passage, Macaulay wrote, "There is not and there never was on this earth a work of policy so well deserving of examination as the Roman Catholic Church." Macaulay's grandiose style of writing history is now out of favor, buried in ideology that looks at the past in terms of a present political agenda. No longer is there the moral imperium for the historian to tell what happened. History must bend to politics, and if it must be twisted, the cost is worth it to achieve political ends. Years ago a friend who teaches both classics and history offered this definition of history, and I have never been able to find a better one: History is the story of great men, great ideas, and great events. Yet I would carry further that definition. Those of us who studied history in college were required to take some kind of course in the philosophy of history. We were taught as part of this course the concept of history among the ancient Hebrews. Although seeing themselves as part of history was essential to their biblical faith, still, we were told, the Hebrews were not historians in our modern sense. Their history was as much myth as fact. We like to think that we today know more about fact gathering than the ancient Hebrews. We can better stand aside from the passing scene and record what is happening.

Yet it occurs to me, as I have sat at my desk and pondered some things, that the Hebrews grasped the main idea of history. They knew the primary source—God himself. God is, as they thought, Lord of history. History is the unfolding of God's plan for his creation. It is the story of his world unfolding through time. That is not to say that history is the same thing as God. History is not God evolving, a perilous modern idea. Rather, history is a drama, with God and man as actors. God is not a Creator who has departed his world. So intimately and presently is he involved with man, his creature, that instant by instant he holds man in existence. One instant's inattention, if that were possible, would send man to oblivion. History is the story of God and man acting in time, in the world. This created world is the word of the Creator, whose nature is to communicate. Thus the world, God's revealed word, is intelligible to man, discoverable by him at least to the extent that he can see dimly through his partial blindness that, because of the Fall, is his nature. History is the story of God's gift of creation offered to us and our acceptance or rejection of it. It is the narrative of what we do with the world we are given. When we say that history is the story of God and man acting in the drama of time, we recognize that because God is an actor—the star performer—the time involved is both human time and the time of eternity. Therefore the events of our world have an eternal dimension. Man, God's creature, in his character, his ideas, and his actions has a transcendent meaning beyond human time. God has lifted his creation to his own infinite sphere. Thus his world has a transcendent character that we can sense but cannot yet fully know.

Because God has given us the freedom to be not puppets but actors in the historic drama, we can take hope that history is not foreordained. Foreknown, yes, but, mysteriously, never prescribed ahead of time. Our freedom really exists. If history has a beginning and an end, a coming forth from and returning home to the Alpha and the Omega, the Lord—then history also has in between a long story that is written partly by us. Within the limits of our abilities and circumstances, both in our individual lives and in our lives in the community, we have enormous latitude. If we use it, we have a freedom already given us by God to improve our situation. We at any moment can change history. Unless we ourselves refuse God's grace, we as individuals are never doomed. Likewise, unless we allow it to happen, our civilization is not doomed to extinction. And the Lord is merciful; he gives us opportunity after opportunity. The tale of every civilization before us is peppered with refused opportunities, occasions when events could have taken another turn but did not simply because people refused to use their freedom to turn away from a path of destruction. We might say, in other words, that these were occasions when people refused to be converted. Thus history is a tale of what we have done with our freedom. Sometimes we have used it well. Often instead we have chosen slavery.

To view the world as a sweep of history, as a dramatic revelation of God, to see ourselves as historical beings with a story unique to us are proper and necessary activities of our intellectual and spiritual life. The study of history, if undertaken in the proper way of looking at how God has pierced human time to live with us, giving us limitless occasions to acknowledge ourselves as his children whom he is trying to bring home, is a discipline that builds in us a knowledge of reality. If we properly study history, we discover that it is difficult to retain illusions about human nature, to fail to see the pull that evil has on us. Yet if we, along with our study of historical context, apply ourselves to the literature of history, especially to the books written by the greatest minds in history, then we are moved by the heroism, the heights that people can attain.

Furthermore, an awareness of history and of our place in it as inheritors of Western, that is, Judaeo-Christian, culture encourages us to consider what we hope to pass on to our children. If we sometimes puzzle over what we can teach them, how we can help them see what the world is, and if we know ourselves to be strictly generalists with a patchy education at best, then to practice an awareness of history simplifies our task. What we do is begin at the beginning. Assuming the unquestionable—that God exists—we move to the first step, the beginning. In the beginning was the Word. In the beginning God created heaven and earth. And so we have the greatest event of world history: God created the world. For Christians the second greatest event of world history follows from the first: God became man and lived among us. Then comes the third great event of history: Pentecost, when the Holy Spirit descended to be with us in his Church. Creation, Incarnation, Pentecost, then, are the facts of our history. These are the objective facts of reality. Now we can proceed, for it is from these three facts that we form our assumptions about the world, about human nature, about our purpose. From the objectivity of the Creation and the Incarnation and Pentecost comes our vision of who we are and what we are to do.

The keystone—indeed the whole of our vision—must be our recognition and acknowledgment that we are the creatures of God. What has angered man over the ages is exactly that he is a creature; he would much prefer to be God. Man has always thought creatureliness a demeaned state. Yet surely God considers creatureliness a lofty state, for he created us for no reason other than that he loves us. There is no reason why we should be here. We do not have to be. It is only that God looks upon existence as a splendid thing. Because he loves us he brought us into this favored condition. Our existence is a gift, a condition that in no way did we cause. As our existence is a gift, so too is our nature. The human nature we are given, with our freedom and our intelligence, is just what we need to receive the revelation of God, that is, the gift of his light. This light we naturally desire and need to break through the blindness that we have inherited from our first parents.

Our response to the gift of life and light that God showers upon us is, if we do not stifle it, gratitude. When anyone who loves us bestows on us a gift, we respond with gratitude, joyful thankfulness. How much more thankful we will be to God, who loves us in boundless excess of any human love of us. Moreover, when someone loves us, we are delighted. We desire to return that love not grudgingly but with a leap of joy. When we are loved, we can scarcely wait to return it. It is true, by the logic of justice we do owe God gratitude for his gifts of grace. Yet when we respond by loving him, we do not think in terms of justice or what we owe God. We think in the language of love—which is to pour ourselves out, to give all, not merely what is owed. Furthermore, when God created us out of love, he was not, in any human sense, just, for he owed us nothing at all. He simply created us because he wanted to. Consequently, our gratitude to God is far more than a fulfillment of justice. It is more exactly our love for the very source of our being. It is our recognition that we are made for God. Human lovers often have the sense that they are made for each other, and no doubt they are. So much more, then, are we made for God. Thus our simplest answer to why we love God must be that we are made for him.

As we ponder what we are to do, how we should live, what we should try to teach our children, our prescription for life will flow from our vision of gratitude for the gift of our creatureliness. If we are made for God, we are made to be with him, the Divine Person, just as we are made to be with the human persons we love. To be, it is often said, is to be *with*; thus our nature is to be with God. Because God is goodness and truth, moreover, then we, too, are made for goodness and truth. Since God, who is good, is our happiness, then our happiness consists in doing the good. As wayfarers, however, our journey toward the good will never be fulfilled during this life. Yet we do move along, inch along, backsliding, but still, through the grace of baptism, Eucharist, and the other sacraments, cutting away a bit of our blindness and self-centeredness.

Our journey, even on the miniature scale of a journey up the Ohio River, is a journey toward virtue, an effort to cooperate with grace to become as good as we can. To be what we are meant to be, that is, followers of goodness and truth, is to acknowledge ourselves as creatures and so to be as fully human as we can be in this life. Our virtue is to be all that God meant us to be, to live in harmony with the being he gave us. And the nature he gave us is one that desires goodness and truth.

God has given us freedom to choose him, that is, to choose life as opposed to death. We do have a genuine choice. What we are given is not the appearance of a choice. But because God is our happiness, we are happy only when we choose God. Our freedom is ours for a purpose—so that we may choose God freely, not under coercion. Yet by the very reason of the kind of beings we are, we become unhappy when we deny our nature as creatures of God, when we try to recreate our own nature and a new standard of good other than the one God has set down.

Our life, which is never static, is an unfolding drama of our movement, freely chosen, toward or away from God, the good. Our freedom is this choice of virtue. Though we are free to move away from the good, when we do we move into slavery. Slavery is not the imposition of a vindictive God but rather what logically results when we choose evil.

Finally, in thinking properly of freedom, we are more accurate when we look upon it not as what we have a right to do but what we ought to do. Our freedom is not to demand rights from God. Our freedom does engage our responsibility. Yet even as we do what we ought, we do the good not because a dictator God told us to do it but because we love God, who made us creatures who love the good. The highest virtue we choose for its own sake. We choose goodness, in other words, for its own sake, for no other reason than it *is* good—and we are meant for the good.

Throughout my undergraduate study of history I had been fascinated by the relationship of freedom and law and of religion and society. Everything I had been reading under the tutelage of my father and the conservative writers, along with the courses and projects I chose to study, pointed up that inclination. For any given historical period I was never so much interested in the details of political, social, and economic happenings as I was in what people of the day were reading—especially what they were reading for their spiritual and intellectual nourishment. What I enjoyed most was what sometimes goes under the broad title of intellectual history, a rather pale term, it seems, for recounting what people of a given period consider worth living and dying for. The themes of God, freedom, faith, family, church, city were some of those universals that wound in one form or another through all times and all places. By the time I was drawing to a close my DePauw years, I in a modest, beginner's way had traveled with those themes from the dawning of European history to the present. I had, however, barely touched on their manifestation in my own country, where they had in some ways reached new heights and had in other ways lost something. Realizing how essential the European background was for knowing America, I also understood that my task lay unfinished. I could not go on to anything else in life without first study- ing some American history. My next step, conse- quently, was a master's program in American history at Indiana University.

Graduate school for the most part was a lonely, dis- heartening experience. In the first place, I was in love and was anticipating being married in a year or so; I would rather have been home in Indianapolis plan- ning a wedding than writing papers in Bloomington. In the second place, Bloomington was gripped by a mid-Sixties pallor and decay. Though unknown to me, Emily Harris and her husband toiled in some basement building bombs. Everywhere were grim faces framed by long, greasy hair. Jeans cut to drag the pavement, beads, and dirty sandaled feet were de rigueur. My apartment was in a dark old house on East Seventh Street, where the front porch was decorated with bicycles, a motorcycle, a baby swing, and a cat litter box, all belonging to various tenants. The graduate program itself was not particularly stimulating, and yet it was worth it for just one thing—the introduction I received from one excellent professor, Trevor Colbourn, to colonial America. Colbourn encouraged me to embark on research on one of the pivotal minds of the American Founding—John Adams. In studying Adams and his world, in absorbing his *Novanglus* papers, his *Thoughts on Government*, his *Defence of the Constitutions*, his *Discourses on Davila*, his letters in old age to Thomas Jefferson, I saw encompassed in one man the moving attachment the Founders had to what was to become America and the brave effort they exerted to frame a government that would ensure a balance of freedom and order. It was, furthermore, impossible not to draw from this study the overwhelming conclusion that the Founders were religious men, implicitly if not explicitly, who held as a point of honor that they were morally bound to obey a normative standard not of human making.

In this sense of obligation to a transcendent order they—sadly, I believe—were in another world from ours. The religious underpinning of the Founding has been to me one of the great revelations that has come clear through the desk. I have come to think that the religious perspective of the Founders has been a contribution to and one of the high points of the history of the Church. As a Catholic, I hope that the Catholic Church can offer enlightenment in these current difficult times when the Founders' religious vision is being denied. Even though the Catholic Church is not institutionally linked to the American polity, it nonetheless offers a religious vision that is highly compatible with that of the Founders, a vision that enhances, deepens, and adds weight and substance to that of the Founders.

Not everyone would agree that America in origin is irrevocably yoked to religion. The prevailing faith today is secular, flourishing under the guise of pluralism, a catchall word that has come to mean, plainly, truth as opinion. Secularism is now engraved in law. The tragedy of this condition is that the Founding Fathers did not envision America in this way.

To be sure, they did not want an established church. They thought that belief could be protected better by separation of the powers of church and state. They had seen, moreover, how low the church can sink when her aims become those of the state.

Yet they had no intention of framing a government under which people would live as if nothing permanent could be known. On the contrary, the Founders staked their lives and their honor on the premise that some ideas are far better than others—that it is better to be free than not; that government should be according to law, not by tyrannical decree; that laws should be fixed and equally applied; that men are not the inventors of morality but are subject to a higher or fundamental law. Though the Founders feared the structure of the "Romish" Church and wanted no such institution in America, they nonetheless were themselves the beneficiaries of the classical-medieval synthesis of Western civilization. Sometimes casting their ideas in the vocabulary of seventeenth- and eighteenth-century compact theory, they did voice some of the vision of the Enlightenment. Yet their philosophical ancestry had far older and deeper roots. Their ties to the classical world went back to Aristotle, Polybius, Cicero, Marcus Aurelius. Their Judaeo-Christian tradition derived from the Decalogue and the Sermon on the Mount. Their devotion to the English common law came to them from Glanville and Bracton, from Fortescue and Coke. From their classical heritage, from Judaeo-Christianity, from the common law, from the documents of their tradition—Magna Carta, the Petition of Right, the English Bill of Rights, the Mayflower Compact, the colonial charters—they assumed a natural or fundamental law of which God was the source and that no king or subject might breach. The most casual look through the writings of the Founders shows how pivotal to their case was the idea of this unbreakable fundamental moral law. There can be no doubt that the Founders, if not all formally Christian, were unanimous in their assumption that religion would be a given of the new nation. That God was the source and end of their freedom they assumed before all else. What they wanted to prevent at all costs was the usurpation by the state of man's freedom to find God. Their suspicion of an all-powerful state was in the highest tradition of Western civilization. The noblest minds of the ages—the men of the Great Books—had opposed the notion that we are our own reason for being. The noblest saw a transcendent end for man, and the Founders joined this company. Always at pains to dissociate themselves from revolution, the Founders considered themselves not revolutionaries but bearers of the tradition of Western civilization, custodians in particular of the English constitution. Again, a cursory glance at their diaries and letters and formal papers indicates how unstintingly they hammered on this point.

Anyone who has read something of the works of the Founders comes away awestruck by these men. How did such a group of people, educated in such a way, come together at one time, in one place in history? In the long course of history such gatherings of gifted men are rare indeed. Americans even today like to think this collection of wise minds and tough characters was providential. I, for my part, unabashedly claim that it was so. For one brief moment a group of men aimed for the highest. The frame of government they devised grew out of their experience, their heritage, and their conviction that man can live freely and virtuously, provided he submits to the controls of a law that refers to a source beyond this world. The Framers made a noble endeavor. Dividing church and state as it had never been done, they took a chance. They knew perfectly well that the new government could not survive without a religious and moral core; they wrote treatises on this very issue. But still they took the risk of separation. Why? How could they be sure they were not dooming the new country to moral collapse? Because they counted on an outside source of strength. Since they knew that a people could not remain free if the state were their purpose for existence, the Founders realized that people had to take their reason for being from outside the state, from a source transcending the state. Hence in a society where church and state were divided, the moral and spiritual vigor that would keep the society healthy was to come from sources beyond the pale of the state. The two strongest of those sources were the family and the churches, bolstered, too, by an array of every kind of private organization and communitarian enterprise. Separated formally, the state nonetheless would be informed, corrected, and invigorated by the moral and spiritual authority of the various churches. Disentangled though church and state would be, the religious vision inherent in the churches still was to be the source of life for the state. The churches were, in other words, the assumption behind the state. On its own the state could have no independent life without becoming oppressive. Thus the only life it safely could have was that breathed into it by a church that would stand outside it. Consequently, even though the Founders disestablished the church in America, they knew that it was exactly the source of life that would keep society vigorous. They intended disestablishment; they did not intend secularism.

But the Founders did not count on a strange phenomenon of our century. They did not expect the church to ape the state. They did not expect the church to abandon her transcendent character in favor of fulfillment of the kingdom of God in material terms right now, right here. In urging the church to do so, both Catholics and Protestants have given up the church's concern for the permanent things; they have joined the assault on truth as its own authority. In effect they have announced that truth refers to nothing objective but is pegged only to consensus or majority vote.

The Founders would tell us today, I think, that the state is helpless to save itself. Since it has no source of life of its own, it must depend on reinvigoration from the institutions that have transcendent referents—the family and the church. The question is, however, will the church recover her intellect in time to save a failing society? Here I venture to speculate, along with others, such as Richard Neuhaus, that, if the Catholic Church in America recovers her recognition of her own purpose, she could guide America to recovery of its soul. The mainline Protestant churches appear to have waned too much to be of help. Besides, their deviation from sound purpose has been more drastic and of longer standing than in the Catholic Church. Judaism probably does not have a wide enough hold on the American population to carry the day. Fundamentalism offers a vision too narrow, too suspicious of the intellectual heritage of Western civilization. If any church is able to infuse new life into America it will be the Catholic Church. And if the Catholic Church can bring this off, it will be what the nineteenth-century New Englander Orestes Brownson, for one, would have expected. There are problems with some of Brownson's ideas, for he, more violently and honestly than many of us, was often in the throes of successive phases of belief. Nevertheless, he was frequently brilliant. As a convert to Catholicism who was also a philosopher of America, Brownson understood far beyond anyone of his day what a great and fruitful alliance Catholicism and America could make—not a formal partnership, to be sure; he was as opposed to an established church as were the Founders—but a bond of common principle. Said Brownson in *The American Republic:*

> The United States have a religious as well as a political destiny, for religion and politics go together. Church and state, as governments, are separate indeed, but the principles on which the state is founded have their origin and ground in the spiritual order—in the principles revealed or affirmed by religion—and are inescapable from them.

Amplifying the essential religious character of human life, he went on:

> As religion includes all that relates to communion with God, it must in some form be inseparable from every living act of man, both individually and socially; and, in the long run, men must conform either their politics to their religion or their religion to their politics.

Since the Catholic Church was the fullness of Christianity, Brownson thought, and America was the highest form of political society yet seen in world history, what grand partners Catholicism and America would be. Brownson understood that America, unlike other countries, was formed uniquely upon ideas—noble ideas. Its Founders, humbly aware of their responsiblity, set out to formulate from their legacy of freedom under law a frame of government. Brownson was convinced that the founding of America was providential. Furthermore, as a Catholic he believed that "religion is not a theory, a subjective view, an opinion, but is, objectively, at once a principle, a law, and a fact, and, subjectively, it is, by the aid of God's grace, practical conformity to what is universally true and real." Thus Brownson, because he believed that the Catholic Church was founded on what was not subjective opinion but on what was universally true and real, had become a Catholic. He thought, furthermore, that the political destiny of the United States was "to conform the state to the order of reality, or, so to speak, to the divine idea in creation".

Brownson would be horrified, no doubt, to discover the degree to which American society is buried in deconstruction, in relativism. Yet, just because relativism prevails as the philosophy of our pluralistic America, we may need the antidote of Brownson's view of Catholicism as the proper partner for American political life. What other religious vision, even considering the present dilemma of the Catholic Church in the West, has such breadth and wholeness? What else encompasses to such a degree the fullness of being? What else, despite its plague of heresies that are simply the result of our fallen state, has hewn over two millennia "to what is universally true and real"? And the hopeful fact of the Church is that in her reality, in her orthodoxy, she still does hew to what is universal and objectively true. In its orthodoxy the Catholic faith, in short, is the hope of the Western mind. That realization comforts us. It reminds us that, for many of us, as for Newman, no other religious vision holds water. Some other visions may be partly right or half right, but none of these branches exhibits so fully and maturely the Lord's vision of his Church as does the ancient, gnarled, scarred—and beloved—trunk of the Roman Communion. For those of us who love it any other vision is unthinkable, illogical, and therefore impossible. We will stay; we will try to remain faithful; we will try to do what the Holy Father asks of us. We recoil at the hint of seizing for ourselves the declaration of what is good or bad, what is true or not true. That was the sin of Adam and Eve. We dread the sin of making our own minds and wills, rather than objective reality, our final authority. We know that if we take to ourselves that authority of deciding truth, we proclaim that God does not exist. And so we pray for the virtue of obedience, which, after all, means submission of our mind and will to what is.

Obedience is not easy today, but then it never has been. The Lord himself told us it would not be easy, that the way of the world is to throw up obstacles to our obedience. We thus become discouraged, wondering if Western civilization can survive its crisis, wondering if even the inspiration of Catholicism can overcome the modern mania to politicize all things and strip them of spiritual content. We question whether the Catholic Church can cure the disease of countless of her own members who are afflicted with this very political reductionism, a disease that must be cured before the Church can help preserve even a shred of the intent of the American Founders. But when we become downcast, we do well to look upon the Church and upon the sweep of civilization in the same spirit as we look at our own lives; we ourselves, by the grace of God, have survived—and not only survived but also often thrived. We see that the Church has survived. We see that civilization, too, somehow survives—not always in the form we expect or hope for, but it does survive. It does not die out. Somewhere there is always a flicker, a candle of hope to pass on to another generation.

Czeslaw Milosz speaks of pockets of virtue as the repositories of civilization. There are always these pockets, he says, and these little bastions of virtue are what keep the highest values of civilization alive for our children. Small comfort, we tell ourselves. How can tiny pockets of virtue prevail against a general moral collapse? Perhaps they cannot; perhaps they will only keep alive a flicker of light. We must face the possibility of failure. We must accept that possibility as a price of the Cross in the world. Further, we must accept that possibility as a condition of our status as people on a journey, as yet unfulfilled. Our call is to be faithful; as he has promised, the Lord will take care of the results.

But we must also pay attention to Milosz' pockets of virtue. They are more hopeful than they first appear. When we begin to look for these little enclaves, we find many more than we expected— and we find them often in unexpected places. When we find them, we likewise discover that their influence is proportionally far greater than their size. We begin to wonder, then, whether it has not always been these small pockets of brilliance, these luminous bastions of ideas, rather than the lumbering mastodon of civilization as a whole that is the actual heartbeat that keeps the race alive. It seems to me that if we are devoted to preserving our Christian culture, we ought to be on the watch for these pockets of virtue, these enclaves of goodness. We ought to collect them and keep in contact with them. They form a network of good and faithful people.

Faithful women, moreover, have a significant service to perform in the formation of these bastions of virtue. Of all gatherings of people the home is the most conducive to making itself a pocket of virtue. A woman in her home, exercising her instinctive role of passing the values of civilization, of the faith, to her children, is in a position of great influence. If she understands what her heritage *is*, what it is she is passing on, she can, with her husband, foster in their home a little community of virtue. To transmit the values of civilization, however, she must know what those values are. She must have an understanding of herself and her family as inheritors both of the larger Christian culture and of the more specific American manifestation that follows directly from it. Thus the two pivots of her intellectual tradition ought to be, first, the classical-medieval synthesis of Judaeo-Christianity and, second, the philosophy of the American Founding, which grew out of the first. If she is to ground herself in these two aspects of our civilization, then the desk will be a focal point of her life in her home. If she is to have any part of making a Catholic contribution to American history, if there is to be such, then she must know what she is about. She will devote prayerful concentration of mind, as much as she is able, to reading the great writers of Judaeo-Christian culture, including some of the best of the Americans. She will encourage her children to educate themselves in the same way. She will take on this task not with the disinterest of one for whom one idea is as good as another but with the responsibility of a trustee for whom the handing over of the patrimony of the civilization is a sacred duty and privilege. She is preparing the next generation for the journey. In the privacy of her home she runs a school and an armory. With her books and Bibles, her admonitions and exhortations, her prayers and hugs, all made tolerable by some treats from her kitchen, she has labored to give birth to a new generation of Catholic Christians. Has she been fruitful? Gingerly, carefully she opens the door of what she hopes has been a little bastion of virtue. She sends forth into the world the first pilgrim to whom she gave birth. Breathlessly she waits to see what will happen to him. Anxiously she strains to see. Then she glimpses him. And, lo, he is standing upright. He even walks forward. But he walks carefully. He is carrying the treasures she gave him.

Chapter V

The Immaculata

Cincinnati, our visitors say, is one of America's more picturesque inland river cities. For two hundred years the Queen City of the West, as Longfellow christened her, has hugged the northern bank of the Ohio River at a point between the Great Miami and the Little Miami, where Ordovician hills form what geologists call the Cincinnati Arch. These hills are mother to civilization in the Ohio Valley. As the hills curve around the undulations of the river, the city in turn curls into their folds.

Neither life nor landscape in this stretch of the Ohio Valley is stark or sharp. By turns tender with the newborn green of spring, lush with mature summer fullness, tangy with autumn apple red-gold, or soft with winter monochrome, the river valley is more shadow than angle, more subtlety than showiness. This is a smallish landscape, not tight enough to confine, but comforting, enfolding its inhabitants in its maternal bosom of hills. Cincinnati is a feminine city, all curves and dimples and encircling arms, her streets rippling up and down, around, changing names from origin to end as lightly as does any woman, whose prerogative it is to change her mind. Contrasted with flat, sprawling lakeside cities of the Midwest—Chicago or Cleveland, brawny and hard-edged—or geometric, grid-patterned Midwestern cities laid over cornfields, such as Indianapolis or Columbus, all decidedly masculine, Cincinnati is a gentle, smiling matron, roundishly full in the sedate dignity of motherhood, welcoming, yet still retentive of girlish freshness and modesty. There is not a single harsh turn in this soft charm, not a bony protrusion anywhere to mar the smoothness of the hills as they wrap the river in circling embrace. There is no dazzlement here, nothing spellbinding or dramatic, but there is much of comfort, warmth, moderation, gentility.

In this pocket of the valley people tend to conform to the hospitality of the landscape. Once here, they seem never to leave, more than a few tracing their Cincinnati ancestry to arrival in the days of ark and flatboat. Although the earliest Cincinnati settlers clustered in the riverfront basin between the hills, when the invention of the incline railway gave the inhabitants access to the bluffs, the population moved from the constraint of the basin into the surrounding hill-sides, arranging their thin, vertical houses on Mount Adams or Mount Auburn or Price Hill.

Autumn is high season for these hills. By September the nights are cooling off, even though the hills stay warm like nursing mothers. During the night a chill breath wins out against warm earth, and in the morning the hills smoke with fog, their silhouette muted until the sun rises high and burns off the earth-bound cloud. October is for these hills their peak of glory, when beneath the sun's radiance they burst into gold. Amber clings to the trees until early November, despite the usual rains that come at October's end and shake loose most of the brilliant show of leaves.

November, though fallish, may yet host a light dusting of snow, but a powdery blanket on these slopes is unlikely before January. December seldom brings much snow; it is rather the drizzly, overcast month. Yet it is also the month in which Cincinnati, maternal, feminine city and quite properly city of the Virgin, is most representative of the Mother most blessed. In this month of hushed waiting, the Advent when with the Virgin we contemplate the mystery of her pregnant womb, Cincinnati's bosom of hills rests in deep quiet, breathing so reposefully that no perceptible rise and fall of motherly breast interrupts the stillness over which a monochromatic mist drops its veil. In silence we, too, like her city's hills, wait with the Virgin. We wait for the fulfillment, and we wait for the signal that will alert us which turn we should take on our journey toward it. This is the Advent hush when, together with Mary, the hills silently ponder things in their hearts. What but silence is seemly when contemplating the God-life in the Virgin's womb?

Only the rhythmic flick of windshield wipers sending rivulets of rain toward the corners of the glass breaks the stillness of a late December afternoon. Driving east on Columbia Parkway out of downtown, I look up through the drizzle at my favorite sight in the city. There, atop the hillside of Mount Adams, stands the plain gray stone church of the Holy Cross-Immaculata, and there at the peak of the gable stands the glistening white Immaculata herself, Virgin of the Ohio, beckoning with outstretched hands. From her summit, where she stands eleven feet high, she commands the best of all views of the city. She guards the steps that run steeply all the way from Saint Gregory Street to her church door—the steps that countless faithful since 1860 have climbed each Good Friday in the Pilgrimage of the Holy Cross. Plainly visible from downtown; from Covington, Kentucky, across the river; from the long stretch of parkway that follows the ridge line of the eastern

hills, our Lady guards her city and her river. Appropriately she looks downstream, toward the end, toward something beyond her. Not for herself does she live but for her Son.

I do not know of another American city where the Virgin rules so prominently. Few American cities have in their skyline a religious symbol as direct as the Virgin. Yet the Immaculata belongs to Cincinnati; she is inseparable from the city's identity. More than that, I like to think, the Immaculata belongs to me. She has become for me the symbol of the end toward which my spiritual journey is unfolding. The slow movement of a life toward its goal, the awakening of a soul to its reason for being are proceeding with and through the Virgin. But to come to that realization of Mary as the fulcrum on which balances the full radiance of Christ has meant a long river's journey upstream, backward toward the source—for in God's simplicity source and end are one. Our river's beginning is also our homecoming. Our Alpha is our Omega. We come from God; we return to God. In the in-between we learn to live in God's life, in his sacraments. To live the sacramental life is to learn the path toward home. Carefully, delicately, Mary our Mother, in the example of her *Fiat*, tends the homesick heart in its love of the sacraments and leads her children home.

On a December day a low sky weights down the

river valley. The river itself presses downstream in a gray swath, slithering between misted hills, finally bending out of sight on its journey to surge into the Mississippi at Cairo. Here at Cincinnati it still has half its journey to go.

A thousand miles the Ohio runs—not much in the scale of twenty-five thousand miles of earth's circumference. Distance, however, is one of the few things we are allowed to think of as relative. Seventeen years ago, when we moved to Cincinnati from Newburgh, that two-hundred-mile trip may as well have been twenty-five thousand miles. I was an exile, banished from home and family and friends. I was a Hoosier girl to whom happiness was nearly synonymous with home, and I did not want to come to this new city. Whether this place was two hundred miles or twenty-five thousand miles from home made little difference; it still was not home.

One year went by, two, three. My husband and children were home, but I was not. My heart was in Newburgh, in our honeymoon apartment, in our Darby Hills house, in our parish of Saint John's. Every visit back to Newburgh tore open the wound of homesickness, each scabbing over as slow and defiantly difficult as the time before. Then a fourth year went by. Rather suddenly the realization came that I was home, a suddenness that I cannot explain. After awhile the symbols of the old home no longer meant what they once did. Without the people they symbolize, the symbols of any home become tired and forced. Their reality in the present trickles away like water; they assume then the reality of the past that can live only in memory. There is no use fighting this hard shift in symbolic meaning. It happens whether we want it to or not. To sustain a life the symbols must refer to being that is present, not being that once lived there. The transition between loss of old symbols and acquisition of new ones is the Golgotha before the stone is rolled away from the empty tomb. It is the loss before the gain, the dying before the rising. Wandering through the new house, seeing the familiar furniture in unfamiliar rooms is the stumbling of a nomad through a city of shattered symbols. There is no resurrection until the nomad begins to make sense of the new surroundings, which means that he is no longer wandering but has reached home at last. The frantic urge to find the sacred in strange, unfamiliar clumps of matter, the strain to discover form and grace in newness that appears awkward and unlovely because unknown, the struggle to swallow the unknown in order to make it known as quickly as possible are microcrucifixions that bombard the pilgrim on his path to discover satisfying symbols. Only when he finds living symbols of the sacred in the things around him does he regain his steady course.

Things, often the smallest mundane things, become symbolic when people we love are somehow attached to them—for example, the cranberry sauce and yeast rolls we make for holiday dinners because Gonga always made them, and everyone loved them. A Thanksgiving dinner without her cranberry sauce and rolls would not be itself—some kind of dinner, but not *Thanksgiving* dinner. A bedroom of two daughters is their bedroom no matter if they are away at school. Yet if they should never come home and sleep in it again, then it becomes something else—a bedroom, maybe, but not *their* bedroom. The Darby Hills house is still dear to us. For years, though, we have been away from it, and so our attachment is no longer a reality but is now instead a memory. As a symbol of our family that house has lost its immediacy. Our present house is now our family symbol. Even though memory has its own sort of life, an existence singular to mankind, and even though memory gives us continuity through time, nonetheless we cannot live on memory for long. Whether referring to the culture around us or to the small frame of our own life, we cannot love a symbol that no longer refers to reality. Flags, pageants, precious documents—like cast-off houses—lose their meaning when the people who once loved them have gone on to some new attraction. Our changeableness keeps us ever checking to see whether the old symbols still mean what they always did. If the symbols have lost meaning, then we suffer from that loss, and we struggle to gain meaning in something else that stands for what we love. This is our human way.

Inseparable from each other like chaff from wheat, our loss and gain, dying and rising are the pattern of our human life. Our lives are made hard not merely so often by what would be called unexpected devastation, such as accidents, untimely deaths, and other disasters, as by the natural separations and losses that are part of normal life. Simply by living and growing older we lose things. Growing up, growing old, sending away, saying goodbye, moving away, seeing our parents succumb to infirmities—these are our experiences of death as surely as our own physical death will one day be our final experience of loss. And yet to every loss in life there is somehow juxtaposed a gain, a resurrection. We send our children away so that they may return with a spouse and children. From all the losses of change come such resurrections as mastering stage fright, completing work, hearing the right man say, "I love you", getting married, having a baby, watching a child learn to walk and talk and read, gathering with family, and realizing that one's parents and children are one's best friends.

In all this search for symbols that mean something, our search is for the permanent thing behind the symbol—the fidelity within the symbol of the house,

the love that will outlast a set of Legos or a Big
Wheel or a Sasha doll, the bond that will tie whether
we live in this house or that house, this city or that
city. The symbols, crucial as they are, pale beside the
real things they stand for—the people, the reality. A
symbol stands for something that is abstract, that we
cannot see, such as a flag for our country, a cross for
our faith, a ring for fidelity. A symbol stands also for a
living thing or person who is temporarily absent, such
as a collar for a dog, a nest for a bird, a necklace for a
girl, a book of photographs for a family. When the
living being is present, the reality supersedes the symbol; when the family is gathered around the table,
they do not need, in order to know who they are, a
photograph of themselves around the table. When
reality is present, we do not need a symbol of it. For
that reason we know that the Eucharist is not a symbol. Christ, the ultimate reality, is present under the
appearance of bread and wine. His eucharistic food is
real, not symbolic. Our search for symbol ends with
the ultimate reality of the Eucharist. Our search ends
with God himself, who is a Person, not an abstraction, and is never absent.

From losing old symbols to finding new ones is an
uneasy groping through semidarkness, feeling along
the damp cave walls, putting a toe forward to check
the ground underfoot, widening the eyes in an effort
to force enlarged pupils to take in the merest ray of

light. How long this queasy quest for firm ground persists depends upon the degree to which the seeker takes on the colors of his environment. If, like me, the seeker lives like a chameleon, sensing almost before looking whether he is amid lights or darks, reds or grays, graceful shapes or heavy ones, he will take longer to cure of homesickness for his old familiar colors and shapes and smells. Until he has wrapped his mind and senses around the new surroundings and taken them to himself, the very newness will send cold tongues of fear licking at the back of his neck and electric shocks coursing unexpectedly through his stomach.

Slowly, though, new symbols began to take shape for me in my new city. Here as well as there were reflections of our Lord, earthly forms through which his divinity could explode. Here, too, I discovered the Virgin, who became for me the symbol of where we are going on our journey. Though she is not the beginning and the end of our journey, she is the means by which we arrive at our home. She is the companion on the journey, guiding us, consoling us on our way. Without her we never could make this journey at all. What happened between the Son and the Mother is the center of salvation, said Hans Urs von Balthasar in his book *The Threefold Garland*. Appropriately enough, von Balthasar thought, God's gracious revelation of himself can be likened to a river. "The river can never be distanced from its source", which is God. If anyone wants to participate in this flowing river of revelation, then he "must plunge into this wellspring, into its inexhaustible mystery", and the mystery is "that God's Word has really opened itself to us, that it has really been received among us and has really dwelt among us, that it has not returned to God alone but together with us. We can see what this means from the relationship between the Child and this Mother. She totally puts herself at the Word's disposition that it may become flesh from her—flesh from her flesh."

The Virgin, my companion, knew I must come to Cincinnati. She knew I could not stay in Darby Hills forever. Without venturing upstream on my journey, how was I to continue absorbing the revelation of why the Lord had blessed me with the gift of his Church? Entwined with that revelation, indeed its very incarnation, were the unfolding of a marriage and the maturation of a family, which needed the long, steady Cincinnati years to come to fullness.

At the beginning of the journey into the Church began also the friendship with my husband. The Lord's way is to speak through incarnate beings; it was surely his way to bring me into the Church through Bill Burleigh. What most attracted me on that serendipitous blind date more than three decades ago were the kind brown eyes with the twinkle behind them. They mirrored a character of rocklike integrity; and, being the daughter of a flinty father, I took integrity to be the greatest sign of manliness. Bill Burleigh was grounded in integrity—that sure honesty, wholeness, and unwavering steadiness that arise only from having one's first principles in order and one's duty clearly in view. He was a man of goodness and mature character, of virtue in the classic meaning of moral excellence as a proper reflection of a man's strength, graced even from childhood, according to all who knew him when he was a little boy, with unusual collectedness. By the time I met him he was twenty-eight. The brown eyes revealed a soul at peace, for he had pruned the vine of his life to admirable simplicity and knew exactly where he ought to go. Picking up his chair and both astonishing and flattering me by facing it directly toward me, he outlined in three crystal points what he aimed for: to be the best newspaperman, the best husband and father, and the best servant of God that he could be. Thirty years later he has been exactly what he wanted to be—an affirmation that the best people are not complex but limpidly simple. Complicated characters are often troubled characters. A pure heart, by contrast, has no need to explain itself.

A woman surely can have no greater blessing than to be wife to a good man. Although it is possible for a couple to be happy together, to respect and like each other, and yet not to be best friends; although marriages of that kind have always been with us, I am not sure I knew that when I married. Best friendship is what I wanted. Only many years later do I realize how blessed I am to have received the best friendship that I hoped for. It can happen otherwise.

Yet it did turn out in God's providence that Bill and I have been best friends. That very friendship is what impelled me toward the Church. Although the Church in history, the Church as the continual fountainhead and keeper of culture, the Church as the inspiration and buttress of civilization drew me initially, it was the Church as the sacramental life that enticed me to become one with Christ in that life. Because I treasured my friendship with my husband, the sacrament that most attracted me at first was marriage. I loved the Catholic doctrine of marriage as a sacrament that could never be undone. A sacramental permanence that built upon and secured the natural friendship of husband and wife was a grace too enormous to be without. I decided I did not want to be without it. We married at Thanksgiving at Saint Mary's Church in Indianapolis, on one of those steel days that suddenly flashes sunlight in midafternoon. The following July I entered the Church, on the feast of my own Saint Anne, the mother of Mary.

Poorly catechized as I was, however, I had a shallow, confused understanding of the primary sacrament, the Eucharist. In retrospect I probably should have been denied admission until I was adequately prepared. Nevertheless, I was in the Church, and having the comfort of at least one sacrament I could understand and love, the sacrament that united me with my spouse and best friend, a sacrament that I understood was to provide grace for all our lives, then I could apply that knowledge of God's grace to the Eucharist, to penance, baptism, confirmation, holy orders, and anointing of the sick. Perhaps after all my backward way of entering the Church was not so shabby. Catholicism is an intensely incarnational faith, which often appeals—certainly so in my case— to the unsatisfied yearning of a Protestant heart to cling to something more substantial. The incarnational cementing of a man and woman in the vow of the marriage sacrament is obvious—the best possible lesson for teaching a novice the ultimate Incarnation of our Lord in the Real Presence of the Eucharist. If marriage is a sacrament of friendship between Christ and a man and woman, it becomes clear that in the friendship of Christ and man carried out as an eternal dying for us and rising for us under the form of bread and wine, the Eucharist is the heart of all the other sacraments and is profoundly spousal. God's spousal friendship with us culminates in the Cross and extends to us in the Eucharist, by which he actually gives us his own life in the form of food that we eat and make part of ourselves. The Eucharist is the heart of friendship, the ultimate testimony that God wants us to unite with him. Baptism, confirmation, penance, and last anointing further seal our friendship with God, and marriage and holy orders are special seals of our friendship with God through specific vocations.

We spent just twelve years in Newburgh. The Cincinnati years that followed them carried my friendship with my husband and with my children to far richer depths. Even though I had thought Newburgh was the whole, it was merely the beginning. If our family was founded in Newburgh, we all grew up in Cincinnati.

The scene of our growing up has been a two-story suburban house, more substantial than the Darby Hills house, more spacious, comfortable, but incapable of escaping completely its origins as a tract house. Much as I was pleased with the fundamental good sense of this house, I from our first day was aware of its pedestrian character. On the afternoon we moved in I stood in the backyard and burst into tears. For this basic box set in a basic half-acre set in a basic subdivision we had given up our creek, our migratory bird flyway, our Virginia bluebells, our proximity to the river. Even though by most standards of house construction we now had a better structure, we had gained little on the scale of charm. Our challenge, consequently, was to inject poetry into a house that was good but prosaic. I hope we have partially succeeded.

In order to accomplish that semi-transformation, the house and I had to become friends. I say "I" rather than "we", because my husband is adaptable enough to fit immediately into any house that is pleasant and comfortable and to find it friendly. I, on the other hand, who adapt only slowly, must discover the human attributes of a house (a house is a human creation, after all) and must listen to what the house wants to say—for a house does talk and can even talk back. To listen means to study its lines, to feel the volume of its interior spaces, and above all to live with the light that constantly shifts across those spaces as the sun arcs through the sky in its seasonal path. To listen to the voice of a house is to watch how the house meets the light, which means in turn how the light softens or sharpens the shadows cast by the sculpture of architecture and of furniture and how the light irradiates or subdues colors. The new house lacked nearly any precious eastern exposure, nor did it have an abundance of the setting sun. What it did do, however, was to meld the bluish light from the north with the full, clear light from the south, which allowed reds and blues to glisten silver and jewel-like in the northern exposure and jolt wide awake in the southern. The house came alive in a new drenching of color, some bold, some soft. Red is indispensable—the color without which I cannot imagine life. Red, though, is such an active color that I like it paired with blue, where it turns a regal cool cherry and loses its orange heat. Reds, from pale rose to cherry; blues, from royal to indigo; and white, mostly in pale pinkish flesh tones, have defined every place where we have lived, and so they define our Cincinnati house. We have never changed that satisfying scheme but have merely repeated it. All colors are beautiful, yet some colors the individual heart greets naturally with a particular leap of joy. Reds and blues are the gravity pull for us.

The Cincinnati house and I became friends not in weeks or months but over several years. My affection for this house—which grew eventually as deep as my affection for the Darby Hills house—matured in the manner that it might in an arranged marriage. Romance was not there in the beginning; yet because the partnership was solidly formed, it provided freedom for affection to take root. Because I had chosen the house for good and sensible reasons, I needed only the experience of family living in it over time in order for the house to become my friend. I had known the heart flutters of eros with our Darby Hills house. I learned with our Cincinnati house that the steady, reliable comfort of philia is a most satisfying love.

The Cincinnati house bent good-naturedly to the demands of an active young family. Designed exactly for bringing up children, it accommodated our family's needs for work, play, and private spaces. It improved upon remodeling. It grew more handsome with new landscaping, which included a fern and wildflower garden thriving beneath the shade of tulip poplars, locusts, and maples.

Here in this house our family settled into the school years, that expanse of time that to children seems timeless but to parents vanishes overnight and after which the adult emerges like a butterfly from his cocoon to begin another generation. The memory of these childhood years lives more vividly in us than nearly any later memory—perhaps because when we are children, the cushion between us and what happens around us is so thin that we internalize our experiences as fast as they happen. Dostoyevsky understood the sacred character of childhood memories that forever after pierce the soul. At the conclusion of *The Brothers Karamazov* he has Alyosha say to Kolya and the other schoolboys:

> You must know that there is nothing higher, or stronger, or sounder, or more useful afterwards in life, than some good memory, especially a memory from childhood, from the parental home. You hear a lot said about your education,

yet some such beautiful, sacred memory, preserved from childhood, is perhaps the best education. If a man stores up many such memories
to take into life, then he is saved for his whole
life. And even if only one good memory
remains with us in our hearts, that alone may
serve some day for our salvation.

Just one good memory, a thought of when we were
noble, or when others loved us or forgave us or educated us, is enough to give us hope and courage
when we are tempted to fear, to selfishness, or to
wickedness. So powerful an education is memory, if
we use it, so entwined with the sacred, that even one
good memory is all that we need in a lifetime. A
good memory is our recollection of God's providential care of us; a store of memories is thus our record
of providence. We draw upon this library all our
lives. For that reason we spend our lives reliving our
childhood, rejoicing in it, or sometimes reliving our
memories so as to heal them. The good memories,
however, ought to occupy us most. Pondering our
good memories is the best sort of gratitude.

I recall hundreds of good memories from my
childhood in the house on Audubon Road. I hope
that our children will recall as many happy ones from
their childhood on Ropes Drive. For David the
Ropes Drive house continued the education of the

Darby Hills house. For Catherine and Margaret, who were but five and three when we moved to Cincinnati, the Ropes Drive house is their primary memory. Here Margaret stood with me to see David and Catherine on the bus on the first day of school in the new city. Here she waited with me until they returned, hugging Catherine, her best friend, hugging David, her mentor and hero.

The school years passed in a blur of Saint Ursula Villa school uniforms—navy herringbone jumpers and white blouses for the girls, navy pants and tie and white shirt for David; of bookbags and roller skates strewn in the hall; of Saturday soccer games; school Masses in the gym; Christmas pageants; music lessons; social studies reports and science fair projects; birthday parties and field trips. The best memories for me were bedtime readings—from Richard Scarry to Laura Ingalls Wilder to Tasha Tudor to E. B. White. Two little dark-haired, brown-eyed girls perched on either side of me in their nightgowns, while I read Tasha Tudor's *Becky's Birthday*. In the room next door David was doing his homework or taking a break to sprawl on the floor with his Legos and Matchbox cars or thinking up a new plan to tease his sisters, most often by throwing their favorite baby Sasha dolls down the clothes chute.

For Christmas one year Bill hid evening after evening in the basement building a Victorian dollhouse.

Then I had the fun of seeing the girls living in a doll-house world—the same world where I had lived with my friend Judy. Two little dark heads nearly touched in front of the dollhouse; two voices murmured and giggled in a fantasy world. When they outgrew the dollhouse, the girls went into the magazine business, designing and writing *Puella*, a thick set of four-by-six-inch pages stuffed with little fashion drawings and copy of their own supplemented with photographs clipped from catalogues. In all there may have been a dozen issues of *Puella*—published about the time, coincidentally, that David entered Saint Xavier High School and joined the band, and Catherine and Margaret first discovered how much fun it was to attend band competitions and admire the boys from afar.

Throughout all the Cincinnati years and inextricably woven into my memory has been the joyful fruit of maturity—the ever deepening ties not only to my husband and children but also to my parents, my brother and his wife and children, my in-laws, my friends. If I cannot imagine my intellectual and character formation without my father's guiding hand, neither can I imagine it without my mother's lighter touch. By instinct and intuition my mother, like my father, is an Aristotelian, a Thomist, and a conservative. When my brother and I were children, our mother exercised a mild but in the long run fairly effective discipline. Not one to impose heavy regulations and punishments, she set up a daily routine of simple order that probably served as effectively as anything else to carry out her idea of discipline—that is, to instill virtue through practice of good habits.

Both my mother and father, however, have achieved their fullest expressions of parenthood as grandparents. My father's wisdom was exactly meant to come to fruition as Grandpa Ralph, when, through the gifts of his natural teacherliness and his finely wrought philosophy, made all the more valuable by accumulated years of experience, he could instruct and counsel his grandchildren. My mother, once freed of the direct responsibility of parenthood, moved rapidly into her favorite mode of being friend and companion to her children and grandchildren. With her inheritance from my grandfather of gentle affability and from my grandmother of enthusiasm for being part of any gathering, especially a family gathering, my mother as Grandma Margaret justly holds her reputation as a fun-loving, youthful woman of cheerful outlook, sweet disposition, generosity, loyalty, and good sense. If there is a family gathering anywhere, my mother wants to be present; not only that, her children and grandchildren cannot imagine having any fun without her. If the car leaves the driveway, my mother's worst penance would be to be left behind, but then it would be a deprivation for any of us to leave her behind. She is our friend, our soul mate, our anchor. Although she and I have not lived in the same city since I married, scarcely a day has passed in which we have not talked by telephone. We chalk up to necessity our high telephone bills. What would life be without talking and laughing over the daily minutiae that constitute life? What would life be, indeed, without the joyous presence of my mother? Lighthearted and girlish as my mother can be, however, her basic outlook is serious. She has duties and obligations, and people are to behave responsibly and with propriety. Family and friends are primary; disloyalty to either would be a terrible breach of her code of honor. In the private world of my mother, family serves as a comfort as well. We alone know she has a shy streak, manifested by her dread of ostentation and her invariable reserve with strangers. For those with that certain shy streak family is a blessed haven without which the world of strangers would be too frightening to face. I should know. I inherited that Walden trait. Driven underground it may be, disciplined, masked, compensated for, but never entirely overcome. For that disposition any form of public life is an effort, a hardship, even a cross. Happiness is the domestic world of family and close friends.

One of the blessings of my adulthood has been my ever growing attachment to my brother and his wife and children. When I was a little girl, my baby brother was the toddler on whom I doted. Now that we are middle-aged, he is still the baby brother on whom I dote, his wife a sister I cherish, his children nearly like my own. No flowering of any bond has been more satisfying, more an extra blessing that I never really expected than that with my brother and his family. The tie between brother and sister, between brother and brother, between sister and sister is not only one of God's gifts but is also a mystery. From the gene pool of two parents might come an endless variety of personalities, appearances, talents. Yet just a few persons emerge, just a few of the possibilities, no matter how many children in a family, and those few are somehow providentially chosen. Whether those few are much like each other or dramatically unlike, whether they are naturally friends or have to work at being so, is mysteriously unexplainable. Nevertheless, brothers and sisters are born of one set of parents, into one family, under one roof. Forever after they are linked, here and in heaven, they and their offspring, generation after generation.

There is also the possibility that in addition to the recognition of these blood bonds, there may also thrive between brothers and sisters a true friendship, ever enriching as the two grow older. Such has it been with my brother, David, and me. There comes a time in one's forties, say, when the fact of a brother no longer seems a happy circumstance taken for granted but one of God's best gifts that, like all his gifts, did not have to be. As we have grown older, so have my brother and I knit more and more together in our enjoyment of each other's variations on the same family theme, of our personalities, gifts, and idiosyncrasies. We have reared our children together, seen life unfold together, sympathized and worried and rejoiced together. As both we and our parents grow older, we inevitably conclude that one day we will be the only two who will bear the memory of our childhood; no one else will recall our mother and father, our grandparents, and the house on Audubon Road in the same way that we do. Dostoyevsky's happy memory of childhood is our precious bond. The day will come, finally, when one of us is gone, when the other will carry that memory alone. Carrying that memory by oneself must surely be a great aloneness, for so much of our identity lies hidden in the memories of those who knew us when we were little, who woke with us on Christmas mornings and crept down with us to find the packages under the tree, who sang happy birthday to us and for us, and who scuffed through autumn leaves with us on the way to school.

My mother-in-law bears that aloneness of her memories. She lives with us now, nearly a century old, the fact of her lonely survival all the more acute because of her keenness of mind. Her brothers and sisters are gone. Pappy Joe is gone. Her focus trains now on the daughter and son and grandchildren who love her, but sometimes that becomes an effort. No one remembers.

"Tell us about your wedding, Grandma Emma", a granddaughter says. "Tell us about your honeymoon trip to Pike's Peak when Pappy Joe fainted and you cried." And Emma relates once again a tale told countless times. Listeners appreciate; still, no one remembers. I know her loneliness. I also know what makes her happy, for she and I have been friends for thirty years. From her storeroom of domestic wisdom she taught me how to be a young wife. She taught me to cook and clean and tried, but did not succeed, to teach me to sew. She and Pappy Joe babysat and loved, as did my own parents, our children. As a model for a mother-in-law Emma has been my teacher. I only hope that I may be such a mother-in-law to the dear young woman whom our son has taken for a bride. Though mother-in-law jokes are fodder for television humor, there is another model—that of Ruth and Naomi. Would that I might realize in some way that potentiality.

As I reflect on my family who are also my friends, I realize in gratitude that these friendships did not have to be. We could be family and get along tolerably without being friends in the classic or biblical sense of friendship as loving each other not for utility but in shared purpose and for the good. The blessing of these friends—my husband, who is my best friend; my children, parents, brother and sister-in-law, nieces and nephews, mother-in-law; my husband's sister, too, and her husband—are plainly and simply gifts. They do not have to be. At the same time these blessed people who do not have to be are also the framework of my life and my world. How blessed I am that to those who are gifts to me I in return may be a gift.

I reflect, too, on my friends, nearly like an extended family, who are in Cincinnati, in Newburgh, and flung across the country. Some of these friends I have had since childhood and college, some since our early years of marriage. Some are friends of our Cincinnati years, in particular those made through a remarkable Sister of Divine Providence and her Scripture study group. Some are friends made especially fast through mutual reading and correspondence and continual conversation. Some are friends introduced by other friends. And one is the indispensable wise and holy man who gives spiritual direction to my husband and me.

That my family and friends are so precious is evidence to me of a development that I rather think is natural in anyone who proceeds along a standard path of developing maturity—but it may be even more natural in a woman than in a man, although I notice it in men, too. As I have proceeded from youth to past the half-century mark, I realize how ever more incarnational my faith and my view of the world have become. Goodness, truth, beauty reveal themselves to me ever more in fleshly forms—in the very people I love—and ultimately, of course, in the God-Man of Jesus Christ. Yet it is the people I love, in whom I see such wonders, who point me, by their very beauty and goodness poured into incarnate flesh, to faith in Christ as the living God. In my teen years I went through a mild stage of Unitarianism. Though I never doubted God, I thought Christ as God himself was a tougher concept to master. Fortunately, my doubts lasted only as long as my inability to pay attention to what was going on in the world around me. As soon as I fell in love and began to discover that my treasure lay in my husband and my family, my friends and my home, I lost all interest in a faith not strictly centered on the Trinity and the Incarnation. My answer lay in the Christian faith, the most incarnational of religions, and most specifically in the Catholic Church, the most incarnational representation of Christianity.

Years ago I was captivated by the compelling truth of the "I am" passages in Scripture. When those proclamations settle into the mind and take root, there is no doubting the Incarnation of Christ as God become man.

"I Am", said Yahweh when he announced his name to Moses. "I Am who I Am. This is what you must say to the sons of Israel: I Am has sent me to you." Who understands the mystery of this great grammatical equation in which subject and predicate are the same? What we partially can understand, however, is that God is the beginning and the end, the origin and the fulfillment of being and existence. In him all things come together. In him all things live and move and have their being. The most striking revelations in Scripture are those in which language, the very gift we have received that makes us able to understand anything of God, is expanded to its human limits and is carried even beyond us to a transcendent realm we cannot see. Such passages are the "I Am" passage, for example, in Exodus; and the greatest of the great, the prologue to John's Gospel: "In the beginning was the Word, the Word was with God and the Word was God", in which the Word, the Second Person of the Trinity, is described as with God and identical with God from the beginning. There are the passages in Matthew and Luke where Jesus asks Peter to tell him who Peter thinks Jesus is—"Who do you say I am?", a question that specifies there is a definite "I Am" but that also asks for a free human affirmation of its existence. There are, further, the passages in John in which Jesus amplifies by way of metaphor what the "I Am" means—"I am the bread of life", "I am the gate", "I am the good shepherd", "I am the light of the world", "I am the resurrection", "I am the Way, the Truth, and the Life", and the ultimate revelation of himself as synonymous with God, the God of the "I Am", when he says, "I tell you most solemnly, before Abraham was, I Am."

Because God is Word itself and reveals himself through words, *what* words we use when we describe God are not only merely important but are also sacred. Through word God touches our minds. He treats us as intelligent beings with a faculty for communicating with him. Thus Christianity is the most reasonable of religions; it relies on our natural intelligence to respond to the grace in which the Lord speaks the word to us. As Christianity is the most reasonable of religions, it is the most literate. Words in our faith are not to be used carelessly or ideologically. They refer to being itself. Those who deconstruct that delicate and precise harmony attack our capacity to think truthfully about God and his creation.

In our incarnational faith our God reveals himself in the Second Person of the Trinity not as a *what* but as a *Who*—the One who communicates with us as one person to another. Given our limitations as beings who first know through our senses, it is virtually impossible for us to love an abstraction. For that reason the Second Person, by the will of the Father, became man, so that we might indeed know and love

God in the flesh, not restricted to talking *about* God as this or that kind of being and to knowing him only as some impersonal conception of truth or goodness. What we have received in the Incarnation of Christ is not a philosophical *what* but a divine friend and lover who addresses and claims us as a spouse. Our bond to Christ is the intimate spousal covenant of matrimony. The more I love my husband, my children, my family, my friends, who are all so evidently part of the Church that Christ loves, the more clearly do I love Christ, my divine Spouse, and the more clearly do I see him in the people I love.

Once again, though, we sensing creatures are dull learners of abstractions. Consequently, to have the Incarnation fully proved to us, we absolutely require Mary. Without Mary's *Fiat*, the Incarnation would not have occurred. Without Mary's *Fiat*, in which she said Yes to the overshadowing of the Holy Spirit, we would not really know what the face of God looks like. The plan of God to show us who he is turned on the free acceptance of one woman. God's revelation depended on her acceptance of his marriage proposal. And in perfect freedom and obedience Mary said quietly, "Let it be done to me according to thy word." At the end of that wedding liturgy, in which the Angel Gabriel addressed Mary with exquisite courtesy and he and Mary spoke solemnly back and forth, the Holy Spirit had taken Mary as his bride and her ovum had been joined to the Holy Spirit in the ultimate demonstration of God's love for mankind. The wedding of Mary to the Holy Spirit is the example to end all examples of the spousal union God has with his creation. In taking Mary as his freely accepting bride, God joined his spirit to her human nature, appearing on earth exactly as we all do, as a helpless newborn. The Savior of the world required a human mother. From the womb of the Virgin, by her milk, the Son of God was born and lived. By the fleshly gift of Mary—womb and milk— the Divine could wed the flesh. So long as Mary bears God in her womb and nurses him with her milk there can be neither Gnostic nor Manichaean nor Arian heresy. Mary is the safeguard of who God is. As long as she retains her place of honor as the Bride of the Holy Spirit, Mother of God, Christ always will be seen in his full glory for who he is— the I Am.

As my life with Christ and in his Church has unfolded, it has seemed that Mary's acceptance is best expressed by Saint Ignatius at the end of the Spiritual Exercises, when he breaks into his Suscipe prayer. Although there are more ornate translations, this is the one I pray: "Take, O Lord, all my liberty. Take in their entirety my memory, my understanding, and my will, all I have and possess. Everything I have comes from you, Lord, and everything I have I give back to you, to be used entirely according to your purpose. Give me only your love and your grace, and I will have everything I need." These are transforming words, I have found. To offer one's memory, understanding, and will—all the parts of one's being—or to attempt so to do is to alter the thrust of a life. To offer one's liberty is to move toward the only real liberty there is—the freedom that lies in doing God's will.

The Rosary, too, has become my prayer. Admittedly, I have been a long time learning to be at home with it, confirming Maisie Ward in her assertion that the Rosary is often the last thing a convert learns to love. Nevertheless, as Maisie Ward describes the attraction of the Rosary, it is "a very intellectual, very civilized, form of prayer". Nothing quite satisfies the soul so much as living with Christ and his Mother through all the scenes of their lives. The Rosary encompasses all of our emotions and circumstances, all of our highs and lows, all of our rejoicings and sadnesses. Moreover, there is a further benefit to the Rosary. Praying with the fingers as well as with the mind is a solid activity, perfect for men who are both body and spirit. The Rosary is an exact fit for incarnate beings.

Most important, following Mary as our model reminds us that although the spiritual life is anchored in our minds, in the intellectual assent that we make to revelation, that life of the spirit must percolate into every facet of our being. From intellectual assent to revelation our faith must move us to fall in love with the Lord. Not only does the Lord ask for our minds when he woos us; he also asks for our total gift of self. Just as man and woman give themselves totally in marriage, so does our divine Spouse ask us to allow him to unite with us in a matrimonial giving of himself to us. As essential as the mind is, it is not complete without the act of the will that is love. As one of the most intellectual of all saints, Thomas More, said to his daughter Meg in Robert Bolt's play, *A Man for All Seasons*, "Finally, it isn't a matter of reason; finally, it's a matter of love." No one has more perfectly than Mary combined the intellectual understanding of God with love for him. No one has known him more completely or loved him more perfectly.

In our living room hangs a small oil painting, dated 1910, by the Cincinnati impressionist John Rettig. The scene shows a snow-covered Mount Adams hillside dotted with several simple frame houses. The trees in the foreground are bare. Far away at the upper left, against a backlight of silver pink, is a suggestion of the Ohio River. If there had been an early snowfall, this could be a December afternoon. At the top of the picture in the very middle, framed between bare branches, silhouetted against the wintry glow, is the steeple of the Church of the Immaculata. This is a small painting, and so my Virgin of the Ohio atop the gable is nowhere to be seen. All the same, I know she is there, guarding her river, beckoning pilgrims toward home.

The Virgin of the Immaculata is a tangible symbol of hope, a symbol I need, for at the end of this millennium the loss of hope is a powerful temptation. Whatever darkness we face—and we do live in a dark age, when not only Christianity but also all religion is denied—the Virgin likewise suffered with her Son. We have cause to think we are living in the age of the Antichrist, when life is no longer sacred, when the youngest and most innocent among us have been cast outside the rule of law and are at great risk of being killed, when words frequently have no relation to truth, when evil is made to appear as good and good is twisted to appear as evil, and we see not only our country but our Church in America slipping into the quicksand of secularism. Our country that once was thoroughly Christian has reverted to mission territory and is in grave need of evangelization. Though church pews are sometimes full, many who occupy them are virtually unformed, bereft of proper catechesis for two generations. Our civilization is convulsed in revolution. Some of its primary pillars, already having begun to crack two hundred years ago, have collapsed in the last half of our century,

leaving the Church as the only institution capable of preserving intellectual, moral, and spiritual sanity. Against her enemies, who would destroy every vestige of religion, the Church must fight with the one weapon she has but which some in our country are afraid to use: truth itself. Amid the wreckage, in which there often seems little recourse against the tyranny of each individual will, it might be a temptation to give up to despair. But in just such a cruel, chaotic world did Mary suffer. She never lost hope; nor can we, for we, as Mary, know who the victor is. Thus, without being fideists, who do nothing, or Pelagians, who rely only on our own effort, we must, while praying constantly, do what we can. We do well to remember that in just such periods of chaos, when the old order crumbles and all is in question, there are sown the seeds of a rebirth. In such periods the faithful must collect and preserve the materials of civilization, the books and artifacts that one day will inspire that rebirth. In the midst of the dying there is already resurrection.

Like early Christians, we strive to encourage pockets of faithful. Knowing that only in paradise will there be unanimity, we acknowledge that, in this strange new world where nothing holds, pockets of the faithful somehow will be enough. Ideas, seeds of faith, have never been mass produced. They thrive in the catacombs, if need be, gaining heart and strength, then burst unaccountably into the light, nearly full blown. Already a network of catacombs, small but vigorous, flourishes in this country and around the world—in parishes, schools, universities, media, religious orders. Surely this network is providential—and surely it is an act of providence that the head of this network is Pope John Paul II.

The springboard of another spring in the Church and in the world will be reinvigorated Christian families. For me strong young families are the clearest sign of hope. As optimism flames most vigorously when fired by incarnations closest to home, so my own family, with its young people valiantly living in the faith, most confirm me in the hope that a renaissance of faith among young people is not only a possibility; it is already under way, a seedbed for whatever cultural explosion Christianity will generate when it will be allowed once again freely to inspire the faithful.

As the third millennium moves closer, I am prepared to be astonished by the movements of providence. Experience teaches that God's providence far outstrips any plans we have, and his mercy exceeds any mere expectation of ours.

In the final decade of the millennium, and just as I approached my fiftieth birthday, the Lord bestowed upon me another of his mercies. We bought the farm at Rabbit Hash.

All these years my life has unfolded within the triangle inscribed at the top angle by central Indiana where it hits the National Road; at the lower left angle by the southwestern Indiana boot; and at the lower right angle by Cincinnati, with the Ohio River underscoring the bottom of the triangle. My life does still unfold within this figure. Now, however, the triangle dips just enough to include the Kentucky side of the Ohio at a tiny place called Rabbit Hash, across the river from Rising Sun, Indiana.

Buying the farm was exactly what we never expected to do. A friend who knew how much we love the river told us it was for sale. We looked on Sunday and bought on Tuesday—eighty-three acres high on a ridge overlooking the Ohio. Steeply rolling and heavily wooded save for a fine meadow in the center, the farm is a haven for deer and wild turkeys. It has two barns but no house. The house will come. At first we thought of a weekend house, but as the splendid view of the river swirling between wooded Kentucky hills and Indiana farmland won our hearts and our imagination, we began to think of building a permanent home. Different from a house that we might have built when we were a nesting young couple, this house will be a house of gratitude and a house for generations, intended not only for us but also for our children, all now nearly grown, our future grandchildren, our parents, our family and friends. It will be a federal farmhouse, appropriate to the Ohio Valley, with wings and lots of windows facing the view, with places to read and pray and cook and feast, to play and work and rest. How grateful we are, how surprised by joy we are that this beautiful spot in the world has fallen to our care, this rolling earthen goodness that gives us promise of spending the rest of our marriage where we began it—on the Ohio River. The first time I heard at close range, after so many years, the hum of a towboat laboring to push its barges downstream, the thrill of recognition in my chest reminded me how homesick I had been for the river and how I longed to continue my journey in company with it. To live once again so close to the river, to wake with it, listen to it, watch it, to respect it in all its moods is something that, although I never expected to find it again, I must have yearned for. To live with the river now seems the most natural thing in the world. That sureness came back with a rush when, long before sun-up one April morning, we drove out to the farm to look for wild turkeys. As we crunched down our gravel lane and up again into the meadow, there, beneath the night sky, our river lay dressed in palest gossamer mist, touched faintly pink by the barest reflection of light dawning in the east. Even in Newburgh we never saw a pink April river quite like that. When morning dawns on the Eighth Day, it surely will arrive as it did on that morning. I was all the more reminded then that, at least for me, there is only one place that most approximates home. That is the Ohio Valley, and the part of the valley that is dearest is the river itself. Happy as I have been in Cincinnati, it was not until we discovered the farm, a mere thirty-eight miles away, that it became clear to me how I had missed a place—a real piece of land, a part of earth. When we bought the farm, my father told me that owning a piece of land was entirely different from owning a house and lot. He was right. It is not the fact of owning property that counts; it is the spiritual attachment one makes to the land and to the place. A house in a subdivision serves a family for a generation. A piece of land is a sacred trust we hold and pass on through generations. Giving one's heart to a landed place is a solemn effort to mark one's spot on earth as permanent and sacred, to recognize the land as another incarnate sign of God's spirit breathing in the world.

There is more time in the country to think. There is more quiet, more continual reminder from the natural world that we are only part of God's plan, not the whole of it. Watching nature unfold steadily through the cycle of seasons concentrates one's sights on the journey we all make, which my husband and I, amazingly, may now continue in company with the river.

Our sense of the journey sharpens in middle age, it seems. The end, though far away, we hope, is nevertheless in view. When a woman's childbearing years end, and she is both helping her children found new families and caring for her parents, who once cared for her, she wonders how her life will unfold in her new role not as a bearer of life but as a counselor and caretaker of life. A new incarnation of God's presence extends before her: a cementing of her covenant with the generations before her and the generations that will follow her. Her mission, as ever, is yet to preserve and pass on the patrimony of faith and culture that has been entrusted to her. The faith, the memory of civilization is hers to keep safe and to keep alive. Together with her husband she cultivates that faith and that memory so that a little band of faithful may survive as a part of the remnant for the rebuilding. Perhaps the farm will be so blessed as to serve as a monastery of sorts, where the family within will pray and work to keep alive the mustard seed. One day, in God's appointed time, the mustard seed, already rooted in fertile soil, will come to maturity.

In a Rabbit Hash winter, when the trees are bare and snow dusts the hills, and the river glints in the light of a cold sun, nothing in this still landscape obstructs the image of the river as the vehicle by which the Alpha and the Omega flow into one. The journey toward home goes on—for me and for my husband and children as for my ancestors who traveled this river a century and a half ago. At noon I hear the Angelus bells peal across the river. The Virgin is here, just as she is in her Church of the Immaculata, guarding her river, urging us to her Son and to our home.

Along the ridgeline the buds of the maple trees are already swollen with hidden life.

We will break ground in the spring.

The Scribe's Epilogue

The historical way of seeing, the scribe believes, is the great contribution of Judaeo-Christianity. God's encounter with man in time, begun in the Old Testament Covenant and culminating in his becoming a man himself and entering history alongside us, put the fundamental stamp on Western thought. It bonded the human intellect with time, making it impossible for man to think of himself as outside of or separated from history. Each person comes into the world at a particular time in a particular place, specifically chosen by God to be incarnated when he is and how he is. The incarnation of each one of us is not a matter of chance. God's assurance, first, that we are known and loved from all eternity, even before our mother's womb, and, second, his entrance into history as a man like us in all things but sin is proof that our existence is not accidental. We are worth far too much in God's sight to be accidents.

Whether we speak of universal history or of our own personal histories, we are not here by chance. No civilization, including our own, has shown up by accident. No life, including our own or that of our children, has come to be by accident. The abiding astonishment of our lives is the gift both of whom and to whom we are given. Yet if it is an astonishment, it is also a gift that is meant to be. The amazing fuzzy-headed newborn, sleepily scrunched in a warm bundle in my lap, with her fat chin propped against my hand and her own little hand resting feather lightly on my arm, is meant to be right where she is. So, too, she is meant to be the sweet, pretty collegian whose gentle brown eyes are now level with mine, who rummages through my sweaters for something to wear, who still moves through life with a light touch. Her younger sister, taller still, once a laughing, spirited toddler speeding around the yard wearing a pink jumpsuit, has grown up to be a vivacious collegian whose dark eyes snap and laugh and who continues to direct our lives. Their older brother, who has towered over me for years, who at age three hummed his small toy cars along the kitchen counter, chatting comfortably as I cooked, has become the reflective, steady, leaderly young man who comforts us all with his good sense and lightens us with his wit. These children—all astonishing gifts who were meant to be—have not grown up to be surprises. The little girl whom our friends called "a little lady" is a gracious, intelligent adult lady. The energetic little girl one friend called our "chairman of the board" is still chairman. The boy who at age three a friend described as "a good gentle lad" is now a good gentle man.

The child who was a surprising gift turns out to be often not such a surprising adult. If we could but see, the potential for the adult person was there from the beginning, waiting only for the person to make the free choices that would allow him to come to his fulfillment. One choice of goodness frees him to make another. Despite mistakes, he grows slowly from choice to choice, one building on another. If he reflects, he can see a pattern in the long string of his choices. This pattern may deceive him into confusing providence, the orderly encouragement of the person toward his end in God, with fatalism, the assumption that because they have to happen, things happen the way they do. Especially if one makes the same mistakes over and over, he may begin to doubt that he is really free.

History, both our own and that of the larger scheme, can be troubling and deceiving. The very way in which events come together, in which they build on one another, sometimes makes history seem determined. For the unbeliever who resists the notion of a living God history is almost sure to be determined. For him it is a forced march into doom.

If the ancient pagan considered the world to be out of his hands and manipulated by fate, then the modern pagan has appointed himself to remake human nature so that history can fulfill the ends that man himself has designed for it. In the second case, however, man takes on a project for which he has no aptitude; immediately, then, he falls prey to the demons of coercion and totalitarianism. His efforts to be his own god, his own ruler and lawgiver, end in his enslavement. Thus, whether he is the ancient pagan subject to inexorable fate or the modern pagan subject to his own enslaving pride, he is faced with a world too much for him, terrifyingly lonely and ultimately unfree. Whether he is enslaved by gods of chance or by himself as god, he knows that neither has real authority to bestow freedom upon him. Thus he lives in an unfree world in which history is not history at all but is reduced either to fate or to ideology.

In contrast, the believer who avoids the determinism of both ancient and modern pagan also understands that even if history is not determined, neither is it a free-for-all. It does move ahead within limits of order. Even if history appears to be chaotic for long periods, whether in the life of an individual or a civilization, it is essentially orderly. That is not to say, however, that one can discover specific laws of history. One would be hard-pressed, for example, to discover unshakable authenticity for Tolstoy's claim that a so-called great man such as Napoleon has merely illusory influence on the course of history.

And one can but pity Brooks Adams in his noble but fruitless search for a law of civilization and decay. All such attempts to divine laws in history generally result in making history determined. The Christian, however, to retain his identity, can never accept an idea of history as determined.

Yet a history that is free is not lawless. Because history is the gift of an orderly God, it cannot be lawless. Nonetheless, the "law of history" is not an external law according to which events must conform but instead is a different sort of law—that is, an order implanted in the very nature of a being itself. No being has created itself; God is its Creator. As a creature it has a specific nature that orders the being toward the end for which it is created; this end is God. Although man is the undetermined being who is created with freedom to choose his end, he is nevertheless created as the kind of being who, if he chooses against God, will make himself extremely unhappy. Although his will is in no way coerced, his being predisposes him to find happiness only when he acts in harmony with God's will, a will that unfailingly wants the best for the beloved creature. In this understanding human freedom is limited—genuine but limited by the kind of being man is. But limited freedom is still true freedom. What may appear to be coercion or punishment by God for choosing against him turns out to be simply human unhappiness over choosing something other than God. And so the law of history is not an external law of determination but the law within human nature itself.

The relationship that God has established with his creatures is intensely personal. Not in coercion but in love he has made everything for himself. Man is made to love and serve God; therein lies his happiness. This law of his happiness arises not from a force arbitrarily imposed upon him but from his destiny of intimate union with God that the Creator himself has lovingly implanted in his soul. Everything in creation is made to fulfill its end in God; everything is made for God. Man, too, is made for God. Though he is free to disobey God, his own happiness depends so entirely on a harmonious friendship with God, who is meant to be his most intimate Friend, that choosing against God violates the deepest desire of his human heart and so violates the very order of his being. The law ordered into the human soul, then, is not a law of coercion but a law of love.

When the scribe of the kingdom records some of the scene of history, what he describes, whether he refers to the life of a person or a civilization, is the response of the human heart to God's overtures. Not everything that happens is truly history. To be sure, in the broadest sense history is everything that has happened. And yet, as Josef Pieper describes it in *Hope and History*, history is not really earthquakes or floods. Nor is it what simply evolves in time. Nor is it most accurately everything that happens to us, being born, growing up, dying. It is not even what we are given by way of intelligence or talent or who may come into our life. No, in Pieper's view our history specifically involves not these incidents and encounters alone but what we do when we meet them. What do we do with the events and people we are given? That is our real history—what we do with the objective happenings of our life.

"The really crucial thing is what we ourselves make of all this", said Pieper.

Both kinds of factor combine to determine the full nature of what actually comes to pass. It is an intertwining, then, of what destiny presents to us and the personal response that we ourselves contribute to this that first gives rise to genuine "human history" as well as to "history" per se in the full, proper, and exact sense of the word. Hence, an event becomes historical when what is specifically human comes into play in it: freedom, responsibility, decision, and therefore also the possibility of willful blunder and guilt. In contrast, precisely this accounts, first, for the essential singularity, the unrepeatability, and the noninterchangeability of the truly historical, but above all for the fact that a historical event is by no means predictable or deducible from things that have already occurred.

All kinds of subtle pressures tempt us to subject history to forecasting and prediction. Since we are people of reason, we quite properly make plans for a probable future. Yet in humility we know that history is not foreordained. Moreover, to know that history is not foreordained is the ground of our hope. But to know that it is not determined does not deny providence and God's foreknowledge. Time and history do belong to God. If God had wanted to make a determined world, he could have. Yet he did not. A determined world would have been founded in force and therefore would have been alien to God. The dramatic free world God gave us, in contrast, is founded in the love that one being only has for another when he gives him his freedom.

The world God has given us is a world from which he is not removed but in which he is instead intensely and intimately involved. His relationship with us is not that of an autocrat. Rather it is the far more dramatic and fascinating one of a lover or a dear friend. In every moment of our lives our intelligence and freedom meet the mysterious and loving intelligence and freedom of God. In every moment God gives himself lovingly to us. His very nature is to give. Giving is what he has done in every split second since the first moment of creation. Though God gives himself lovingly to us, our response to him may or may not be loving. Even with his grace, our response is free. Thus history is not predictable. Only God's love is predictable. The turn of events that will result from our interaction with God's love is no more predictable than is the turn of events that results from our acting with the human beings who love us. Two free intelligences acting together produce a drama, not a computer program.

God has given us our raw material—our genetic inheritance, our family, our circumstances, our traditions, our freedom. Acting freely within the limits of these gifts, we do things that produce unpredictable results. Our history is indeed undetermined.

As part of his grace God gives us one thing more: time, the medium in which the results of our response to God unfold. Revelation has told us that God intends for us one day to be with him in heaven. Consequently, if we ourselves do not obstruct the end and if we allow it to be fulfilled, we know what the end will be. We have been told, moreover, what our proper response should be to the offer of God's grace. What we have not been told, however, is how each of us fits into God's loving plan to achieve his end. Although we know *that* we fit, we cannot know *how*. The how is behind the veil.

Why are we given time? Surely God could have

created a world in which we would enter not as babies but as fully mature adults. Surely in such a world we could have been spared the suffering of our bumbling immaturity. But then in such a world of maturity we would also be created ready only to die. And we would have no chance to learn to love God; we would arrive in the world already loving him. God, however, prefers the world he created. It seems he is so opposed to coercion, to forcing us to love him, that he saw fit to create us as beings with a potential for loving him rather than with a love already fulfilled. He must think it a far better thing that a being not be made to love but be free to choose to love the God he may gradually see is more and more beautiful. God's way, then, is to woo his creatures over time. He is a courtly and courteous God, not a tyrant. His way is that of the divine Spouse.

Our history plays out in the expanse of time between our creation as potential lovers and our eternal fulfillment of union with our beloved divine Spouse. We live our history on two levels. The first is the level we ourselves see, our efforts to take the opportunities we think God is offering us and to live humbly, wisely, and prudently. The record includes both our successes and our failures. Then the second level is that of God's hidden meaning. This level, of course, we do not see, though we do have a sense that it exists.

The scribe knows that it exists and trembles before it. At this secret hidden level occurs the intersection of God with us in time. Here, veiled and unseen, occur God's whispers to the human heart. Here is offered the divine revelation that we are as beloved to him as the Son is to the Father of the Trinity. What he offers us in this secret beckoning is none other than the same life with him that he enjoys among the Three Persons of the Godhead. At any given moment, then, even in the millionth fraction of a second, God intersects with our lives in time. Because we cannot escape time, God does it for us. He sends his Son in the Incarnation to join us in time, to show us what time is for, why we live, and for whom we die and rise again. At any given moment, in the secret unknown depths of our hearts, the horizontal lines of our lives are punctured with the dazzling vertical thrust of the Lord's grace. The horizontal line of our lives extending through time is simply a series of minute and continuous points intersecting with grace. Were it not for God's ever-present grace, in fact, that at every second holds us in existence, we would simply explode into annihilation. But God does more than simply love us into existence second by second: he guides us.

We often speak of God's providential care. The question is: How does providence work? Not by force; we know that. Not by God's making our

decisions for us. Not by appearing to us as so overwhelming that we are obliged to love God. No,
providence, I think, works in a way different from
that. We have received our genes, our family, our
circumstances, the facts of our incarnation. We are
given, too, our freedom. And then we are given
time. Time is the medium through which we exercise our freedom. Slowly, very slowly in time we
learn to love God, to obey him, to do his work. In
time the gifts of our incarnation can be sanctified by
love. All this occurs, however, only in time—not
outside it. Since we cannot step outside of time,
then Christ comes to be with us in time, gently,
gradually showing us what our gifts mean. It is
through these very concrete gifts, riveted in time,
that our grace comes. The little fuzzy-headed baby
at the breast, for example, came into my life as a
surprise and a wonder, as all life comes. I looked at
her and loved her. I began to take care of her and
teach her, and then my history with her began to
thread its way into the tapestry of time. Our graces
of providential care come to us only within time.
Christ comes to us to sanctify every moment of our
time. Our time is our precious gift. Every moment
means a renewed chance, by way of the specific,
concrete things we are given, to choose Christ and
love him by doing his will. Every moment means a
chance to move closer into his life. Every moment

means a chance to move further toward our true happiness.

There is an opening prayer of the Mass for the seventh Sunday of Easter that sums up time and history:

> Eternal Father,
> reaching from end to end of the universe,
> and ordering all things with your mighty arm:
> for you, time is the unfolding of truth that
>   already is,
> the unveiling of beauty that is yet to be.

When we were young, we may have anticipated that if we could just read and study enough, eventually we might be able to grasp the meaning of history behind the veil. There is no doubt that without this search for the meaning of our history, we cannot tolerate our lives. We are creatures made for meaning. We cannot stand the thought of ourselves as just here. Nonetheless there comes a time in life, I think, when the struggle to grasp meaning becomes less an intellectual exercise and more a surrender of the intelligence to the divine Presence. There is a relief in realizing that in both the life of a civilization and the life of a person real change and real progress occur almost secretly, at the level of the hidden in history, at the point where the invisible divine Presence meets the human soul. It is at this level, unseen by the outside world, where the impact of divine

grace, made known in some way to the human intelligence, has opportunity now to soften and change
the human will. It is at this hidden level that man can
make even the feeblest fluttering of will toward his
Lord, and his divine Lover will greet his movement
with yet another outpouring of grace.

We can take comfort, furthermore, that if we try
to live our lives as charitably and wisely as we can,
we are doing what God asks of us. To do our part we
need not, as we may once have thought, understand
the whole picture. Though our understanding is limited, God uses us anyway. As Newman said in his first
Meditation on Christian Doctrine:

> God has created me to do Him some definite
> service. . . . I have my mission—I never may
> know it in this life, but I shall be told it in the
> next. . . . I have a part in this great work: I am a
> link in a chain, a bond of connections between
> persons. He has not created me for naught. I
> shall do good, I shall do His work; I shall be an
> angel of peace, a preacher of truth in my own
> place, while not intending it, if I do but keep
> His commandments and serve Him in my
> calling.

When we ask why we are here and how we may
fit into God's plan, we seldom receive any direct
answer. Perhaps someone much advanced in the

mystical life may come close. My own experience is simply that when we ask the question of why and how and what for, we are shown not mystical visions but beings in the world, concrete beings that we are to love, cherish, care for. Along with the gifts of those concrete beings, we are given time in which to love them. God is not, however, mysterious in a way that leaves us ignorant of him. He does want us to know him; his nature is to bring us toward him.

The mystery of our lives, it seems to me, what our history means, where God is leading us, is explained most satisfyingly and fully in the Mass. If worship of God is our highest activity and the Mass is the pinnacle of worship, then the Mass is the greatest event in which we participate. Yet our understanding of what really happens in the Mass takes more than a lifetime. To finish what we cannot have time or light to understand in this life is a great argument for eternity. One Mass does not explain much to us. An occasional Christmas Eve or Easter Vigil does not effect much in us recalcitrants. But Mass after Mass, day after day, week after week, year after year does do something to clear our heads and improve our vision—these quiet daily Masses especially, round and round through the liturgical year, taking us through the life of Christ. Gradually it sinks in on us that on those winter mornings, when we venture out before the sun is scarcely up, when tree limbs creak with cold and our breath hovers icily before us, we go to meet our Christ, who has burst all boundaries of time and space to come to us. After a while we know nothing so clearly as that we must rush toward that Presence, where our history surely begins and ends. All the stumbling, running feet of the centuries meet there in that Presence, in that burning, searing Sacred Heart that loves us. All the millions of pilgrim feet converge in that incarnate Heart that has broken through tears and time to include us in the loving sacrifice of his Passion. My feet, too, run there, and the feet of my ancestors. All the feet, too, of the children who will descend from me. Slowly, we present pilgrims, as surely as did our ancestors who went before us and our children who will come after us, begin to see something dimly through the veil. Behind the transparent veil we see the glowing Heart.

"The love which the Son bears to thee, a creature", said Newman,

is like that which the Father bears to the uncreated Son. O wonderful mystery! *This*, then, is the history of what else is so strange: that He should have taken my flesh and died for me. . . . Did He not love me so inexpressibly, He would not have suffered for me. I understand now why He died for me, because He

loved me as a father loves his son—not as a
human father merely, but as the Eternal Father
the Eternal Son. I see now the meaning of that
else inexplicable humiliation: He preferred to
regain me rather than to create new worlds.

There is a monastery of perpetual adoration where
I sometimes drop in to pay a visit. The traffic of the
busy thoroughfare outside sets up a steady backdrop
of noise. I mount the steps and open the heavy door
to the chapel. Behind me the door clicks shut, and I
have entered the hush of an eternal present. There,
beyond the strands of sunlight on the marble floor,
the monstrance rests upon the altar. Therein is contained the Presence that sanctifies our world of time
and history. All being exists for that very Presence; all
being exists simply to be loved by Christ.

Acknowledgments

The front cover art is by Edward T. Hurley, a Cincinnati artist (1869–1950), and is used with permission of W. Roger Fry.

The back cover photograph of the author is by Robert A. Flischel, Cincinnati, Ohio.

The frontispiece and etchings on pages 15, 20, 34, 104, 163, and 196 are by Edward T. Hurley and are used with permission of Joan Hurley O'Brien, the artist's daughter.

The author is grateful for the assistance of Randy Cochran in reproducing the Hurley etchings.

62 — wound
61 nursing